Thank You, Cancer? Who even says that?! My wife and I had the privilege of being up close and personal with Danny and Raffi through a small part of their journey. Even the title of this work is but a glimpse into the beautiful way that they held their hearts through one of the most difficult life experiences a family can walk through. After reading this, you will find yourself thanking your cancer too for giving you what breath alone cannot: perspective.

- **Jaye Thomas,** Philanthropist

The story of Danny and Raffi will inspire you and impact your heart! Raffi conquered suffering by showing love to others! Her love for Jesus, her family and others continues today.

- **Gary Kuzmich,** Author of *The Heart of the Courageous*

I miss my friend Raffi so much. To hear her voice again through *Thank You, Cancer* is as heartbreaking as it is beautiful.

- **Liz Wolfe,** Author

Live long enough and life will get messy. Sometimes, it's really messy. Sometimes what we need is the resilient story of those who have lived alongside us and have fought the good fight. Reading Raff and Danny's story has inspired me to press on and stay the course no matter what, because ultimately God is faithful to meet us wherever we are, walk with us in the highs and lows, and no matter what comes our way, stay with us to the very end. Even when life does not go at all the way we want, we have Hope, and Raff & Danny point us to that Hope incredibly well by telling us their story.

- **Cory Johnson,** Lead Pastor Austin Life Church

Thank You, Cancer
A Story of Love, Loss & Hope
Copyright © 2025 DANNY LESSLIE

This book is a work of nonfiction based on the author's personal memories, interpretations, and experiences. While every effort has been made to ensure accuracy, certain details, events, and conversations may have been reconstructed or adapted for narrative purposes.

The publisher and author disclaim any liability or responsibility for any actions taken or not taken based on the information in this book. The views expressed herein are solely those of the author and do not necessarily reflect the views or opinions of the publisher or any affiliated parties.

No portion of this book may be reproduced, stored in a retrieval system, or transmitted in any form or by any means—electronic, mechanical, photocopy, recording, scanning, or other—except for brief quotations in critical reviews or articles, without the prior written permission of the publisher.

First Print Edition, 2025

Cover Design: Rachael Mitchell

Softcover ISBN: 979-8-89514-036-9
Ebook ISBN: 979-8-89514-010-9

While the author has made every effort to provide accurate information at the time of publication, neither the publisher nor the author assumes any responsibility for errors or changes that occur after publication.

Scripture quotations taken from the Holy Bible, New International Version®, NIV®. Copyright ©1973, 1978, 1984, 2011 by Biblica, Inc.™ Used by permission. All rights reserved worldwide.

Scripture quotations are taken from the Holy Bible, New Living Translation, copyright ©1996, 2004, 2015 by Tyndale House Foundation. Used by permission of Tyndale House Publishers, Inc., Carol Stream, Illinois 60188. All rights reserved.

Lyrics from "Don't You Give Up on Me"
Written by Brandon Lake, Michael Fatkin, and Benjamin William Hastings
Used with permission from the authors.
© 2021 Bethel Music Publishing / Brandon Lake Music / Maverick City Publishing Worldwide / Music by Elevation Worship Publishing.
All rights reserved.

Raff,

We were Magic.

CONTENTS

In Their Words	ix
A Word from the Authors	xi
Sweatsuit Dance Party	1
Coffee, Alpacas, and Happiness	7
She Pulled the Pin and Handed Me the Grenade	11
"Be Known for the Way You Love"	17
Goodbye to Dreams	21
Sex is Off the Table	25
Same Side of the Table	29
A Forced, Needed Break	35
It Tore Through Her Skin	39
Parkour!	45
Blessed By Cancer	49
Unwelcome Adjustments	51
She Danced	55
Behind the Curtain	59
Nipples out of Nothing	65
He Held Her Head	75
Gains	79
Violated and Degraded by TSA	85
Cedric	89
A Glimmering Beacon	97
Mama, It's Beautiful	101
October - Change of Course	105
We Move Together	109

Deer Conversation	113
Here We Are	115
Life is So Good. So, So Good	121
December	127
Death and Rebirth	137
Coincidence? No Chance.	141
Emptiness and The Filling	145
Lou Lou	149
Lifelines	151
Unlayering	153
September - Disorienting Grace	155
Silence	161
Energy and Trauma	163
Joy and Love	169
Grace, and Grace, and Grace	173
The Mirror	179
Discussing a GoFundMe Again	181
She Loved Denim	189
The Salt River	191
Crash Cart	195
Evidence of Disease	205
Back, But Not Home	207
When I'm all they have, they'll have all of me	217
The H Word	225
Beauty in the Heartbreak	231
Disorienting Reality	237
Love Transcends Death	245
I Wasn't Afraid to Die Anymore	255
Final Request	261
With Gratitude	263
Bring Danny to Your Next Event	265

In Their Words

I'm Danny and Raffaella's oldest child. I'm going to share a memory with you. My age currently is 10 years. This year without my momma has been so hard. These last 5 years too. I hope this memory that I write makes you happy, sad, joyful or more. Let's start with the memory ok. So at the time we got a puppy, and my mom was like "I'm never letting Lulu in my bed." Lulu was the puppy. Next thing you know it's like 10:00pm and I wake up hearing my dad laughing, so I get out of bed and my mom is holding Lulu, the puppy, in BED. So I thought that was a funny story. Thank you for reading, bye. Hope you enjoy the book. - **Rue**

This story is about my mom. We've been through alot and it's really hard without a mom. She fought for so long, and she chose to fight because she knew that she wanted to stay with her kids and her husband a little longer. She's went through so much, she's been in the hospital, and it hurts to not have her by my side. But she lives in my heart forever. Bye Everyone. - **Ace**

A Word from the Authors

First of all, a heartfelt thank you for choosing to read this book.

As you read, imagine yourself at a campfire with friends. It's you, me, and my wife. All bundled up in cozy warm jackets, in the glowing warmth of the fire, holding our favorite festive beverages. We are going to share a story with you, a love story. One of struggle, triumph and loss, faith and growth born out of a battle with cancer. It's nothing less than extraordinary. It's our story.

There are individuals in this life who are unmatched, one of a kind. Raffaella was one of those. Her friends called her Raffi. She was Raff to me. She was magnificent. A wondrous woman. The quintessential mother. My best friend. Our souls were in lockstep. I was fortunate to walk side by side with her for more than 12 years. I will forever be grateful for that time.

As we embark on this journey, the text will free flow just as an informal conversation among friends would. My words are in full margin. Those in bold are Raff's original words, unedited, which she wrote throughout this journey. I am no grammar wizard, and there are errors that I purposely left untouched. Some of my writing was real time, in the moment, and some was added when I wrote this book. Because time tends to dilute our experiences and our memories fade, I believe the original writings hold an experiential element that cannot be recreated.

There are also words set apart in shaded boxes. These were moments that almost always defied explanation. What seemed impossible became a reality. And, often the reality was much bigger than what we could have imagined or even hoped for. Maybe at first we had passing thoughts that these were just coincidences. I don't remember. But at some point, as more and more totally unexplainable solutions popped up, it was hard to attribute it all to coincidence. There are many, many examples; 10, 20, 30 or more that we documented. It was clear there was something aside from coincidence. Without question, these were orchestrated somehow. Dare I say supernaturally? We began to think so. And, eventually knew without question that God had intervened. We started calling them our "Jesus Moments." They seemed to pop up at every turn. We just looked at each other, smiled and nodded. They were a constant light that drew us forward. As you read, judge for yourself.

My goal was to take this patchwork of our writings and piece them into an emotionally-connected, intimate, insight-filled journey as we navigated those years. Something I only fully realized was possible in looking back.

I hope you sense that Raff is here with us at our campfire, that you palpably feel her presence and our love as you read these pages. I hope you laugh and cry as you read. I assure you, as these words found their home on each page I was doing both. Just as she was one of a kind, our relationship was a once-in-a-lifetime type. She was my person. The light of my life. I really hope that I was some of those to her. I believe I was. Unanswered questions can be heartbreaking. Lastly, I hope that our story splashes brilliant colors on this canvas – this book that chronicles our journey.

May this story, our story and experience of heartbreak but also pure JOY, community, love, deep deep healing, parenting through chronic illness, marriage in the face of a heavy diagnosis, freedom in acceptance, the reality of a cancer diagnosis in America—-may all these topics and conversations bring light.

| 1 |

Sweatsuit Dance Party

I couldn't take my eyes off her. She was mesmerizing. The way she moved to the music. The music was emanating from her, and her movements were creating the whole dance party. At that moment nothing else mattered, everything else diminished. She was enchanting. I'm still undone to this very day.

One year prior to the dance party, on a beautiful day in sunny Santa Monica, CA, I was coaching a fitness class under a magnificent line of towering palm trees on a 100-foot bluff that overlooks the Pacific Ocean. An idyllic location. If there was a place made to view sunsets, this was it. A buddy and I ran a program there for more than two years which eventually grew into a full scale gym in Venice, CA. But, that's a story for another day.

I had moved to California with the dream of starting a gym. Burned the ships, as they say. I left my midwestern hometown in the Kansas City area and headed for the coast. I was all in. Everything I owned was in the back of my pickup truck. I was beyond excited. It didn't even bother me when I saw unsecured items fly from the back of the truck or when I hit a hay bale. I pressed ahead, following a dream which I would be blessed enough to realize. However, there was another more important story that would unfold, and lead me down its very own beautiful path.

It was on a typical morning on the bluffs that a new student came to class, nothing unusual about that. What was unusual, very clearly, was this beautiful soul was different. Immediately, there was wild chemistry between us. There was one particular moment I will never forget. It still makes me laugh. Raffi was her name and as she arrived for class I noticed she had a carseat in her car. Now, we both knew the storm that was brewing inside each of us, but neither mentioned anything of it. It was like this shadow game that we knew was happening, but we chose not to engage.

I nonchalantly mentioned the carseat to her, when I asked if she had kids. She told me she had a daughter, and instantly, all of me was crushed. It felt like the floor just dropped out from under me and everything came crashing down on top. I thought this could potentially mean she already had someone in her life, and that I had no chance. I was SHOOK. Apparently, visibly. Because, seeing my distress, she started to laugh hysterically. She didn't have a child. She was just lightning fast with her wit. She knew the hope that was hanging behind my nonchalant question about the carseat. She was so quick on her feet, and it was so playful. I went from completely deflated, to completely smitten in that moment. She got me so good, and so much of the exchange that took place didn't even require words. We just understood how good she had gotten me. I was never the same.

Months passed. The park program transformed into a full scale gym housed in and all around an old auto repair shop on Lincoln Boulevard in Venice. It was in those months that my whole life transformed, as well.

Of all things, it was a sweatsuit dance party where our story really ignited. That night I had squeezed into a tight yellow velour onesie with a raccoon tail collar, and slipped into my pink Chuck Taylors; because that's what you do, or that's what I thought was awesome. The perfect finishing touch was my handlebar mustache. In spite of what some may say was my WORST look, it was this night that would change my life for the BEST. Maybe I had one or was it 17 beers that night, too? I don't know. At some point, I became mesmerized, and it was something that still dismantles me.

I saw her dance. It was as if the music was coming from her; it was as if her movement was creating the whole dance party. There was nothing else that mattered to me; nothing else had any vibrance. She hypnotized me. Then, from somewhere deep inside of me came all this ambition or confidence or maybe it was just luck; but, I made a choice, and it turned out to be the best thing I had ever done. As they say, with 20 seconds of insane courage I gathered enough gumption to just lay one on her. A kiss. One random, but not totally random kiss sealed it. And, soon, we officially became an item. Within a few months we were talking about children and the rest of our lives. There was no courting period. We knew we had flipped a switch that could not be flipped back.

In 2014 we married. In 2015 we had our amazing daughter Rue, and in 2016 we had our amazing daughter Ace. We both had tremendous communities of people. Raff had managed a BBQ restaurant in Venice for years and was teaching in the school system; and by that time I had built the bustling gym in Venice. The restaurant and the gym were just blocks from one another. The sheer volume of racks of ribs and beers I consumed during that time was astonishing. Well, who could blame me? I could hang out with the love of my life and have the best dinner. I'll always remember that was where she told me she was pregnant with our dear Rue. Life was good and we were having the time of our lives. However, in spite of it all, we knew we didn't want to raise our girls there. So we decided to leave Los Angeles. And, so the adventure began.

It was 2017. We bought an RV and named her Talulah. We remodeled her for a few months while we planned our escape. We literally sold everything we owned, cars and all; and we downsized from a 2-bedroom apartment and stuffed everything we needed plus four people into a 36-foot RV. We lived at the beach for a month during our last days in Los Angeles. There will always be a special place in my heart for the songs of Chris Stapleton blasting on the radio, steaks on the grill, the lapping of the waves, the sun setting over the water, my girls running around and laughing, and my dear love bebopping around, smiling in the sunset. We shoved off from LA with plenty of tears and well wishes from friends, having no idea of the adventure that was in store for us. We traveled for 40 days all through California and throughout the Southwest destined for a small town in Kansas. The amount of stories were endless, but there was one in particular that I want to share with you. It may seem random for now.

It didn't take us long to learn the logistics of RV living. For one thing, each time we drove Talulah into a parking lot, due to her size, she had to be maneuvered to the back of the lot. She looked like a city bus and it was a time-consuming ordeal just to stop for an item or two. Once we found parking space, we had to navigate the long walk to the door with kids in tow through the parking lot congestion.

So, it was during one of those stops, as we walked the customary 100 yards to the store, that this random lady came running across the parking lot and stopped us. She literally was waving us down as if we forgot our kid or something in a shopping cart. I have no idea where she came from. Random town, random stop, random lady. We stopped to hear what she had to say. "I just wanted you all to know that Jesus is with you." That's it. She wanted us to know Jesus was with us. We didn't know how to respond. We didn't even know what to think. Our whole lives were up in the air. I parted ways with the gym, and Raff had quit her teaching job. We sold our cars. Everything we owned was packed into this 36-foot RV. We had two young children.

We were moving to a small town 1700 miles away with no jobs. We were absolutely, irreversibly, as they say, full send. Were we crazy? Was this the right thing? Was this the wrong thing? What if this? What if that? So much doubt and apprehension about the future. We were constantly on edge. And, then this random lady has a message for us. "Jesus is with you." We weren't sure why, but when we heard her message we felt incredibly relieved. We felt we were right where we needed to be. We didn't totally get it, but we knew it wasn't about totally getting it and having all tomorrow's answers. It was about taking care of matters today. Being present. And, we were swimming in it.

"Have I not commanded you? Be strong and courageous. Do not be afraid; do not be discouraged, for the Lord your God will be with you wherever you go." Joshua 1:9 [NIV]

| 2 |

Coffee, Alpacas, and Happiness

We landed in Kansas at my parents' little hobby farm outside of Kansas City. We didn't have jobs, we just had each other. Time to reinvent and make a new life. We lived in that RV for a year. Raff worked a few jobs, and I stayed home with the kids. It was in this season that I learned to love cooking. Switching roles really gave us an appreciation for what the other person deals with. I will forever praise mothers for the mountain of tasks and emotions they manage on a daily basis at home with the kiddos.

During these months, Raff had developed Crohn's disease, a type of inflammatory bowel disease that caused belly pain, severe diarrhea, and fatigue. It wreaked havoc on her body. The stress of everything was too much; and there were days she was on the toilet bleeding no less than 15 times. I had picked up odd jobs including an erratic schedule packing trucks at UPS in the early morning hours. Not my favorite.

I have to be honest, not everything we did back then made perfect sense. We had much to figure out, like jobs, vehicles, and a home; so we might have been a bit premature when we bought two alpacas, but they were great. Those beautiful, gentle animals brought us a special kind of joy. Ellie was white and Foxy, who was pregnant, was our dark female. Immediately we found ourselves discussing names for the baby. Our oldest daughter Rue came up with the name Coffee Bean. And sure enough, when the baby was born, of the 22 possible alpaca color combinations, the baby was brown as a coffee bean. The fleece on her body was a bit lighter than her nose and feet, just as a coffee bean. Somehow Rue just knew it. She didn't know how, but she knew; and, it came as no surprise to us. She seemed to have some kind of a weird clairvoyance. We had witnessed it numerous times and it was becoming a pattern.

Our lives seemed fine and well as we settled into life in the Midwest. At least, to an outside observer. However, deep down Raff and I each had separate battles that were taking their toll. I was panicking on the inside, trying to keep my cool, worried about our next move and our future. And, unbeknownst to us, Raff had her own battle brewing deep inside.

One morning, as we were out and about with the kids, we made a coffee shop stop. Coffee shops had become our happy place. Nothing like sipping a warm beverage in the local purveyor of caffeination. It had become our thing as you will see throughout our story. So here we are, Raff wasn't working at that point, and I was hating the UPS job. No home, no vehicle, no plan and basically no money. With all this weighing heavy on my mind, I mindlessly thumbed through the little local free newspaper. There, I saw a small ad with the solution: Ranch Manager. And, it wasn't just a job. It included a salary, a four-bedroom house on 17 acres, and a work truck. Keep in mind, we had little income to speak of, no vehicles, no permanent place to live, two little kids, a small alpaca herd, and Raff was very ill. That little ad in the free paper that morning had something for nearly all of our needs! I could not believe it, and I could totally do it. I called the number, got an interview, and weeks later I was on the job. What an incredible gift! Dare I say a blessing? Without a doubt, we thought it was another sign that we were on the right track.

"In their hearts humans plan their course, but the Lord establishes their steps." Proverbs 16:9

We loved those days on the ranch. It was 2019 and Raff was able to get her Crohn's under control by researching and applying natural health remedies. Seemed she was always a wizard at healing. When she was younger, she had polycystic ovary syndrome [PCOS] and she was able to find a way to overcome that as well.

Ranch life gave Raff an opportunity to shine. Be her best self. Natural living, outdoor space, gardening, homeschooling, livestock, the beauty of nature. One of her many gifts was that she was a mother through and through. Motherhood was laced into the fiber of her being. She and the girls were just swirling with happiness. When you looked at the three of them, it was hard to tell where one ended and the other began. During the days while I managed cattle, drove tractors, fixed fences, and mowed hundreds of acres, Raff was mom of the century with the girls doing homeschool groups and just living a life we loved. Everything seemed to be humming along. It was no surprise that a favorite ranch activity was accumulating animals. Our alpaca herd grew to nine. We added two ponies who were lunatics, and a calf who was orphaned on the ranch, basically a huge dog. We added dogs and cats, rabbits, and chickens.

At one point we purchased a utility trailer and transformed it into a wondrous coffee shop, the Cowboy Coffee Post. That was a family project. We worked together and absolutely loved every minute of it. The girls were three and four years old and worked the window and took orders. The fall was busy with weekend bookings then a big event with Kansas for Health Freedom where we got to serve Del Bigtree who Raffi always loved. That was a really huge day for us.

Then came 2020, which was pretty trying for us on all fronts. Raising two wildfire little girls became a challenge when they were homeschooled and activities were limited because of COVID. Raff had the girls full time, I worked full time, and we had coffee trailer events on weekends. So our peaceful, idyllic rural life wasn't always restful. For years, our nights were either painfully restless or our sleep was interrupted by the girls. This meant that many days it was a struggle to function at full capacity.

| 3 |

She Pulled the Pin and Handed Me the Grenade

Early that year, Raff had detected a growth, a weird growth on her vulva that quickly turned into a fast growing situation. We had no diagnosis as to what it was. There was only speculation and urgency for removal. The doctor said, "You need to get this removed right now." And, surgery was quickly scheduled for a few days later. The doctor explained that one of two things would be done depending on what she encountered when she scrubbed in. She was either going to perform a vulvectomy or a radical vulvectomy. Radical is obviously the more aggressive version. That was basically all we knew.

Surgery was an enormous leap for Raff. She didn't take medicine. Never had. Drugs were not an option. She had two babies without any drugs. Also, Raff found doctors' visits very unnerving. I can't count the number of doctors' appointments which ended with Raff hyperventilating and in tears. To make matters worse, I could not go with Raff to any of her appointments during COVID. She received all the news

Thank You, Cancer

alone as I sat in the parking lot and tried to keep myself busy and my mind off the screaming reality of our situation.

Raff's immediate family had come into town for surgery day and they were all at our house that morning when I drove her to the hospital. We were scared. Really scared.

Fortunately, for this procedure, the hospital at least allowed me into pre-op, that tremendously awkward time before she went into surgery. It was cold, everything was sterile, masks galore, and nerves couldn't be higher. When the pre-op time ended, Raff was wheeled to surgery and I was ushered to the waiting room, undoubtedly the loneliest place and assignment ever. Sit and try not to freak out for three hours, the whole time consumed by worrisome thoughts of her being fully sedated and then enduring the unimaginable surgical procedure she was facing. There were layers of horror to it. I don't know how long it was, but it seemed an eternity.

When they finally called my name, I was escorted to a little office with a couch. I was unprepared for what was about to be dropped on me. The doctor arrived and started describing the surgery and what happened. She was very clear that they found cancer, the growth was squamous cell carcinoma, and they had performed the radical procedure.

Gut punch. Stomach drop. Time stood still. I was absolutely shocked at what she said. l asked her if she was going to tell Raff. She said no, I was. I almost threw up.

WHAT?!?!

We didn't know this was part of the deal. We hadn't even really discussed cancer. I was speechless.

HOW?!?!

With no medical background, how could I drop this bomb on my wife?

She Pulled the Pin and Handed Me the Grenade

I had never felt more unprepared and unqualified. I guess it hadn't struck me that Raff wasn't going to be there for this conversation, and what that might entail. I was horrified to say the least. Nothing prepared me for that moment. I told the doctor it wasn't fair; that I couldn't answer all the questions and it was unreasonable to put this all on me. But that was how it went down. She pulled the pin and just handed me the grenade. So here was this bomb I just got to hold. She said that she would follow up in the next week with a phone call. I thought, *Oh great, I'll just sit on this grenade for a week. No. Big. Deal.*

About thirty minutes later, flushed, clammy, sweating, eyes full of tears, I was called to recovery where Raff was beginning to wake. She was still so out of it. Actually asleep. Then barely awake. Ever so slowly she began to wake up, but she was not mentally with it at all. She kept asking how it went, what the doctor said, all the things. I just held onto my bomb. I knew this was not the time. I didn't know when the right time was, but it was not when she was in an anesthetic fog. The minutes crawled by so slowly.

She continued in and out of sleep during the one-hour car drive home. I dodged questions, and continued to hold the bomb. When we got home, of course her family had all kinds of questions too. I just kept holding the bomb because there was no way I was going to tell anyone before I told Raff.

Finally, about 8:30 that night it was clear to me that she was fully awake and mentally with it. Again, she asked, "What did the doctor say?" The scene that follows is seared in my mind. I sat there knowing I had crushing news for the love of my life. It was torture. I can't put into words the weight of that moment. I don't ever want to hold onto something like that again.

As I sat on the bed, I began to cry. I told her it was cancer. It killed me to tell her. She was broken. I was broken for her. Each millisecond knifed my soul. I'll never forget the realness and heartbreak of that moment. Writing and reliving it literally turns my stomach. She was looking to me for hope, she was looking to me for safety, and she was looking to me for love. And what I had to deliver was a dagger. Horrible, just horrible.

According to her surgeon the growth on her vulva was originally 1.5 cm by 2 cm. However, she now had a hole, nearly golf ball sized, at 4.5 cm by 2.5 cm by 3 cm. As the pain from surgery began to set in, profound heart ache came with it. The recovery was long, both physically and emotionally. We had crossed into a whole new chapter of our lives and everything was now different. Our lives were shaken to the core.

Aug 3 2020
"In August of 2020, my husband uttered the words, "It's cancer." I lay in my bed at home, unsure as to what happened in the operating room. The one sure fact being that our lives, and my body would never be the same."

It took me months before I would go to a doctor to check this thing on my vulva. I knew better but trauma is a beast. I only trusted one woman to complete a vaginal exam and she lives in California. Robyn Pool caught both of my babies. She walked me through both prenatal periods, witnessed my challenges and victories during birth, and held me through the postpartum period as I processed the birth trauma that made a home in my body.

There was only one person that I could trust to move through a vaginal exam with the care that I so needed as this lesion on my vulva began to uncover the parts of me, unhealed. She wasn't in Kansas City. I couldn't fly to California. So, I waited. I tried to talk myself into going to see an OBGYN so many times. I asked for recommendations, I called around, I waffled back and forth. I called Robyn. I still couldn't get myself to go. The thought of someone else touching me without understanding all that had happened, made me want to throw up. I knew better than to wait, but I couldn't move.

When pregnant with my oldest, Robyn and I spoke about my past with sexual abuse. I felt that I had addressed it and did not see it being an issue in birth. The birth of my oldest was beautiful and I roared like a lioness to push her out. I also ended up with a third degree tear as it was a slow and steady labor until she pressed play to Johnny Cash's "Ring of Fire". Robyn sutured the tear the best she could, as I couldn't stand being touched in that moment, as it brought up feelings related to past trauma. Robyn knew, she met me at my home and we began to process some things together. More healing continued.

| 4 |

"Be Known for the Way You Love"

This quote is in remembrance of Raff's dear grandmother who we lost in 2019. She was the epitome of these words. Raff told me it was a goal she strived for in her own life as well, to be known for the way she loved. The funny part was, Raff couldn't possibly have exuded this more. If you had the pleasure of knowing her, you know exactly what I mean. She gleamed when she smiled and she welcomed everyone with loving arms. Her eyes even smiled. Our daughters and I were constantly showered in love. She effortlessly gave so much. Sometimes I think it came with a cost. Her health was constantly her center of focus. I can't even tell you the number of days she woke up and didn't feel good. It was easier to count the few good days because there weren't many. Yet unless you were close, you would never know. She carried on, loved on everyone, and expected nothing in return.

She probably read more than 25 books on cancer and miracles, and spoke with a zillion doctors. She was in pain all of the time. Bear in mind, she gave birth to two children without any drugs, so when she actually admitted she had some lymph node aggravation, the pain must have been intolerable. Walking and sitting were challenging, let alone going to the bathroom. Yet, she homeschooled our girls, and was an amazing wife. She would rarely ask me for help even though I worked close to home and was relatively available. There was no relief for her. The candle burned at both ends and in the middle. Each day was really hard. Some days we survived by the minute. I remember someone asked me how she was doing and the only thing that came to mind was, she's not crying. We ran the gamut of emotions many times a day in our house. The girls felt it and acted out which made a bad situation worse.

I'll never forget those early days, when we just had no idea what was coming for us. There was nothing quite like the gutting helpless feeling I had as I laid in bed, physically exhausted, but unable to sleep. I tried to calm my racing thoughts. *Am I losing my wife? How do I do this without her?* Then I would hear sobs from the bathroom as she got ready for bed. Weeping in the bathtub. I can't convey the helplessness I felt most of the time knowing that there was nothing I could do to help her. That was some kind of torture, and it happened more nights than I can remember.

The scariest part was accepting that this was a journey that really may not have an end. *How long would it go on? How bad would the pain get? What's next?* It was honestly hard to think past the next hour most of the time. And, I couldn't even begin to fathom the financial piece. The financial weight of it was tremendous for her and for us. The bills stacked up. I couldn't even think about making a payment on the bills because the math didn't work. The financial ramifications of this were terrifying. We were on a single income, and there weren't extra pennies in the couch. To be honest, the pain and just getting through the day seemed to occupy our whole being.

We were very slow to share any of this as we were completely overwhelmed in our own household, hearts, and minds. When Raff finally said she wanted to post on social media I couldn't have been more thrilled, simply because she could offload some pressure. This diagnosis, this pain, this thing was so heavy on her. It was all consuming all the time. She couldn't even sleep. Thankfully many people offered to help, many reached out. That meant so much.

| 5 |

Goodbye to Dreams

The next month or so was recovery, and she was beginning to move around again. We were so hopeful that the cancer that had been removed was our only encounter with all of this.

We were taking our coffee trailer to local events as a family, a really happy time for us. But after a few months, it just became too much, so we took advantage of an opportunity to sell it and say goodbye to a dream we were living. It was very sad, but we knew it was the right thing to do. Cowboy Coffee Post had a new owner. Despite the sale of the coffee trailer, coffee time still held a special place in our hearts. It was our getaway. Our time together. A warm drink, some laughs, the four of us just swimming in the moment. These dates were cherished. Now, when I have coffee, it's like a portal to my beloved Raff.

Other days, like today I feel less overwhelmed and so at peace knowing that even though the girl's worlds have been rocked—

we still get moments like this where **Papa can do an impromptu reading lesson on a napkin while we enjoy a warm drink together.**

Little things. Eye contact. Moment to moment.

There was more heartbreak that year. Losing our white alpaca Ellie was really hard to stomach. A few months later our dear Coffee Bean who had been born on the ranch passed away from the same sickness as Ellie. It made matters so much worse that she was pregnant when she passed. I just about lost it. I was so overcome with sadness. First the cancer diagnosis, then losing Ellie, and then Coffee Bean along with the hope and anticipation of a baby alpaca. It was just too much. In our grief, we chose to sell the entire herd which was crushing on many levels.

In a period of months we had said goodbye to multiple dreams that were just teeming with love and life and our wild adventurous spirit as a family. We choked on the reality of our new path which was becoming more apparent by the day. We clung to each other the best we could, and tried to smile in the storm. But the writing on the wall seemed to be haunting us at every turn.

In spite of all the heartache though, our lives had a crystal clear simplicity to them. We were literally forced to embrace every moment. We moved slowly, we moved as a unit. During this time we got a second dog, a little red heeler named Ginger who did not move slowly but brought some much needed distraction. We already had a beautiful Livestock Guardian Dog CeCe, a very chill Pyrenees and Saint Bernard mix who Raff was just in love with. Ginger became Cece's sidekick but was probably more of an annoyance.

Leave it to your three year old to remind you that everything is beautiful, it's all about perspective.

Me: okay baby, all done wiping.
A: Mamma!! Look!! My poop is so beautiful! Look at the colors!
..and we just think it's some sh*t in the toilet.

To my girls who see and feel it all, I never thought I would be bracing myself out of pain when you run to me for comfort or play. I never thought I would have to limit my physical embrace or adjust the way I comfort your cries, your hearts, fears, dancing or movement with you.

My heart cries and my guilt floats to the surface when we talk about "solutions for my bump" or you witness Papa giving me injections in my belly. I never want you to internalize these moments and carry them with you though, I know that is a path I can't completely control.

My girls who love so deeply and care so much, who cry with me and make me laugh while we cuddle in bed and talk about everything.

This is the human experience. I cannot shelter you from it all but I promise to tread lightly and unveil it with joy, laughter, strength but also the reality of sadness.

This is a moment in our lives and we adjust. We dance in new ways and cuddle in new ways, and find new things to do together and we go to meetings not doctor visits, we create health and turn from illness.
We push through, together. It seems so complicated for us adults but I know for you it is simply love, simply together with love.

| 6 |

Sex is Off the Table

Well this is interesting! This is not a playful suggestion that we are without a table or have a creative place to throw caution to the wind when the littles are sleeping. It was a dose of reality that had encompassed the last year of our lives. Raff had a radical vulvectomy. Then cancer metastasized to her lymph nodes in her groin, so this is where we found ourselves. At the risk of TMI we were the type that enjoyed such endeavors, in fact, over the past decade I believe we were improving and were becoming aficionados of the art.

Being married was for sure a multifaceted pursuit. There were many things to focus on, all of them leading back to what mattered most. Intimacy. Intimacy was where it was at. Someone once simplified and pulled the word apart for me: in-to-me-see. That helped clarify what this overused and under practiced word meant. Allowing each other in was tough, being available emotionally, sexually, spiritually for each other took some doing. Vulnerability in hopes of someone else returning the favor is an exhilarating place to find yourself. That was really living. If we were not willing to go first, we were not playing.

So what did we do in our case? Were we still married? Yes! Were we still in love? Yes! Was there intimacy? Yes! How? We found plenty of options under the intimacy umbrella, as many as 12 options actually. The five that really rang true for me were physical, emotional, experiential, intellectual, and spiritual.

I saw intimacy as a wheel divided into five sections. One section was physical, another emotional, the next experiential, and so on. When I rated each of the five sections according to how much I felt it was present in our relationship, zero [or nonexistent] would be in the center of the pie, and 10 [or overflowing] would be a full piece of the pie. Then, if I imagined the wheel rolling; three zeros, one five, and one two made for a bumpy ride in my intimacy wagon. All tens are smooth but probably a bit unrealistic. All fives or all sevens would produce a smooth ride and energetically was much more attainable.

I say all this to illustrate why life was pretty bumpy for us at times, but thanks to the various intimacy options, we were able to shift around and keep the fire. Physical intimacy is by far the most popular, and this is where we find our ol' stand by, sex. Sex is intimacy, yes. But, physical intimacy is more than sex; it includes touch, massage, closeness, etc.

Emotional intimacy was also an available category. Creating a "safe space" for each other to divulge our deepest fears, thoughts, dreams, complicated emotions, and the like was part of this version. We had plenty of crying and hard talks that really did wonders for keeping us close. They were by no means easy, but self exposure was deeply satisfying.

Experiential intimacy came from sharing experiences and working towards the same goal. This cancer journey rallied us all around Raff towards the most important goal. We could talk for days about stories here. Experiential intimacy was something as small as cooking a meal together, or traveling, or training for a race. Spending dedicated time with each other brought us closer. All four of us were constantly looking for a chance to forget the weight of the situation and just enjoy life. Thankfully we eventually learned to laugh at the craziness of the whole deal. Making light of the struggle really seemed to draw us closer to each other. Those tough times were inextricably woven into the tapestry that was our relationship.

Intellectual intimacy was really helpful as we had to discuss treatments and mortality. Having the ability to share our opinions, emotions, and beliefs in a safe space with no judgement was key to feeling welcomed and loved. It was no secret that we didn't always have the same viewpoints on things, after all I married an Italian woman. But in all seriousness, we were both a tad stubborn and hard headed. However, we allowed each other the space to speak about our point of view which helped us to move forward in a more cohesive and loving manner. And to be real honest, when we tossed egos out the door and changed what we believed, it became a pretty enriching experience. After all life was really about learning and loving, and in both we had plenty of growth to do.

The last form of intimacy I want to mention was spiritual intimacy. This was a great one. Raff and I came from very different religious backgrounds. I came from a Christian upbringing, and she came from a much more worldly place. When we got married, I remember considering whether this was a problem for me. I knew that she was my soul mate, regardless of where her beliefs landed. I wasn't about to let her go. Her experiences were her own, and absolutely should have shaped her. My experiences shaped me. I am no person to pass judgment on someone else. She was definitely more connected to her spirituality than I was to mine; I was a bit lackadaisical with my faith for whatever reason. I guess I was just trying to stubbornly do it on my own. Spiritual intimacy was not only expressed in our faith; we shared the wonders of nature and marveled at them together. We experienced sunrises together, shivered in the cascading water of a mountain river, and basked in the majesty of a mountain range. That generated spiritual intimacy.

Once cancer came on the scene, it seemed there was a complete loss of control for both of us. I noticed my wife began to pray daily, and I began to pray more. We talked about faith and Jesus daily. There are so many instances where we had no doubt the Lord was with us on this journey. I'm talking plain as day examples woven into our interactions with others that leave no doubt that He had us in His hands. Moments that seemed to be written by the author of all this, that wove into our experience. They quenched our hunger for why, and dried our tears, and held our hearts. For this I am eternally grateful. My faith was stronger, my marriage was stronger, and her faith was stronger.

I am not writing this because I am an expert. We struggled all the time. Endless trial and error gave us those moments. We rode through this together and that made us both stronger. We were forced to look for other solutions due to the circumstances. I encourage you to consider the wheel on your intimacy wagon, too. Is the ride smooth? Are you allowing yourself to be seen? Are you holding space for your partner to be safely seen? Just a couple thoughts.

| 7 |

Same Side of the Table

As the months rolled on after surgery, our path began to reveal itself a bit more, and not in a good way. It was in October of 2020 that we began to see the beast rear its head again. The cancerous lymph node on her left hip began to enlarge. At first it felt like a lima bean, and then a little bigger and more uncomfortable as the size kept increasing. You could literally see the change from day to day. It was terrifying, and horribly painful. Raff went from being able to walk and sit, to laying all day, barely able to get around. We got the results of a PET scan which confirmed the cancer had metastasized to her lymph nodes. We needed radiation and chemotherapy, and we were back in search of answers.

For a while, we had chosen a more holistic approach. We used a variety of therapies, from mistletoe injections, ozone infusions, and high dose vitamin C infusions. We definitely saw some success, but then the pain and growth began to outpace the progress.

Thank You, Cancer

My sister and I always say, "Lemons are life." One of my fondest memories are when Danny and I took Rue to Italy for the first time and we sat on the roof with lime and lemon trees. We have so many memories around lemons. So many meals eaten with lemon, so many drinks helllooo Limoncello but also lemon water.

After the diagnosis, I started diving into as many natural, dietary habits I could implement in our daily life. Essential oils became a huge part of this journey-even more so, L E MON.

Lemon essential oil is an adaptogen. That's right. Like the mushrooms we hear about everywhere- lemon, is an adaptogen. It gently detoxes your body, it lifts you up, and mellows you out-it adapts to you. Most importantly in my life at the moment, it doesn't like cancer.

Two things I do these days:

- a whole lemon, and whole garlic bulb in a blender. Drink a shot a day. Put the pulp in the freezer as ice cubes and use for cooking or a snack.

- Lemon Essential Oil in my water throughout the day, in almost anything really. A quick sniff and drop on the wrist too!

Lemons are life.

There were so many things to think about at this moment. Operating from a sound mind, while balancing fear and exhaustion was challenging. Input from the outside was intended to be well-meaning, but in reality it was also based in fear, which really ended up bringing more tension than relief. I speak from the experience of walking with a person in that place. I have no experience with cancer, so I was very humble about my opinions, and tried to be supportive but not add pressure to the situation.

Part 1 :: I have been reflecting a lot on the cycle of pain-> negative emotions -> pain -> more negative emotions that can occur for people living with chronic illness, chronic pain, or who are dealing with heavy life situations.

I used to be in the thick of that cycle, and I continuously chose to stay in it. For whatever reason it was serving me in some way (leave that for another time). This week that cycle was creeping into my life and I had to actively CHOOSE the inputs in my life.

Part 2: When we are in that cycle, it takes a conscious decision to move out of it and break that mofo thing. I know when I am in it, like this morning and a lot of this week— when I feel it creeping and my headspace going negative, I ask myself "How do you want to live your life?" and I act accordingly.

Your inputs matter. What do you allow in your space, in your body- food, music, people, physical activity. Here are some examples and suggestions.

- gratitude list/journal
- 10 deep breaths w/affirmations or prayer

- **high quality food**
- **lots of water**
- **sunshine**
- **get out in nature, barefoot if possible**
- **the people around you**
- **music (make a hype playlist ahead of time to play whenever you need)**

Cheers to breaking cycles

There were so many twists and turns on this path. There were so many moments of growth and moments that tore at the fabric of our hearts. It had all started with urgent surgery for removal of a growth. The surgery seemed to be a great success and it was such a promising day. Then there was the slow recovery. The daily march to getting well. Walking, standing, sitting, laying were all painfully uncomfortable. It took many weeks to get back to where normalcy was somewhere in sight. Moments of pain drug on for weeks, now months. Lying in bed all day went from here and there to every day. You can imagine the elephant in the room when we were parenting little children and Mama was resting at all hours.

My list of responsibilities was endless: cook, nurse, husband, father, courier, cleaner, etc. And I had it easy, I wasn't the one in pain. Raising children, working, and keeping some thread of sanity for each of us, made even simple tasks such as grocery shopping monumentally hard. It was so simple to find myself frustrated with the moment, frustrated with the cancer, frustrated with our situation, frustrated with our crazy children when Mama was trying to rest. She was also frustrated beyond belief as well, as she should have been. Keeping our frustration aimed in the right direction was a learned experience. It was easy to get after each other. Not helpful. We were a team against this cancer, and we had to keep that thought at the forefront and support each other.

Maybe my most profound realization was from those moments of frustration. My sole aim became: stay on the same side of the table.

Amongst the flurry of emotion, the torrential exhaustion, the financial struggle, the pain storm that she was in, the logistical nightmare I dealt with, if we could just be on the same side of the table we had a chance. Without that, I don't think we would. Keeping our relationship healthy and united was always our focus.

There were times I took a much needed moment for myself. Whether it was five minutes with a kettlebell, a hot shower, or a walk to the mailbox. Those moments were vital. I needed them. Also, I was thankful a million times over for all the support we received. For those who phoned, those talks were a lifeline. Every little bit built me up and left me wanting to reach out with big hugs. Hugs from me. Hugs from all of us.

As a man, a father, it was easy to just take it all on. We are looked to as models of holding it together. We are praised for being unaffected. We are raised to conquer. Well, here I am, crying again. I am here, I stand here, I won't let up, I won't relent. At all costs, I will follow through. I was proud of my ability to carry on, my ability to move forward beyond struggle and beyond emotion. But d*mn it, I felt it. And, I don't mind saying so. It hurt daily. The struggle was real. I knew, if you don't expend the surge, you will break. I was close. I overflowed with gratitude, but constantly welled up with sadness. I could feel my heartbeat in my neck. The heartbreak coursed through my veins, and moment to moment was our reality. And the hope? Well, I saw it everywhere.

Cancer aside, we had never been more alive. Figure that one out. Go all in now!

| 8 |

A Forced Needed Break

By December 2020 our life was at a fever pitch. It felt as if we were sprinting just out of reach of the flames trying to consume us at all times. I was running as fast and furiously as I could, too terrified to stop. Ranch management on a 750 acre ranch involved a long list of tasks written on notepaper everyday. It was always considerably more than a full day's work. My job was managing cattle which meant constant fence repair, castrating, mowing, garden work, clearing trees, and all other farm related chores.

One day in early December, fence repair was top priority because the cattle had again found a way to escape. For those of you who aren't familiar with the fence repair process I'll explain. Fence posts are driven into the ground manually with a metal driver, a hollow metal tube that has a heavy solid metal top. All totaled, it weighs maybe 30 pounds. The driver is gripped by two handles, one on each side of the tube. The open end of the tube is positioned over the top of the fence post, and with tremendous force, the driver is slammed down forcing the post into the ground. Heavy work, but simple enough, as long as you keep in mind that metal posts have studs on one side; and the driver must not hit those studs. But that is exactly what happened that day. I slammed the driver down, it hit the top stud and snapped back striking the top of my head with full force. I felt a lighting bolt go from my head to my toes and to my fingertips. I took a knee, and then laid down with my face in my hands.

At that moment I felt my phone vibrate. When I reached for it I saw my hand full of blood, a lot of blood. I knew I was in trouble and that I was going to pass out and had to act quickly. I was working in the middle of 750 acres. I worked solo. No one knew where I was, and I could not be seen from the road. My choice was simple, drive out or bleed out. I crawled into my truck and called Raff who was laid up in bed recovering and couldn't help me; but immediately told me I couldn't come home because it would scare the girls. So off to urgent care I drove. Maybe not the safest, but in my scenario neither was passing out and dying on the ranch. I remember that I turned left at the main light in town and a cop turned in front of me. We made eye contact and he must have seen that my face was streaked with blood, but oddly enough he just continued on. At the urgent care, I passed out minutes after I arrived. Eight staples and a few hours later, I was back home in bed next to my queen.

There was no arguing, I think God forced me to take a much needed break. He knew I had a hard head. Thankfully.

By the way, I do have a Braveheart-esque photo we'll save for another campfire chat.

So incredibly thankful that Danny did not pass out on the Ranch alone after he split the top of his head open, while building a fence. 8 staples later he is home and as Biggie wants nothing to do with Papa right now, Smalls is all about it!

We've had a lot of uncertainty and changes from hour to hour this past week and a half but we C LE A R L Y get the hint to rest.

Therapies have begun this week and we are excited to see progress and healing.

You can go ahead and add Danny's stapled head to the prayer list, please. And someone send the bubble wrap.

Dec 8 20
This past week was my first week hitting treatments everyday. My body was TIR E D, in a way it was a blessing that Danny hit his dome with an iron and got staples so we could all be home.

In my head I had this idea that because I wasn't diving head first into all allopathic treatments, this would be easier— and side effects wouldn't be so bad. That is true in some respects but either way, my body still has to do work to heal, a lot more work than it has in the past and Lord knows we have healed so much leading up to this wild adventure.

Thank you to everyone who has contributed in all sorts of ways. We wouldn't have been able to explore our options as easily if not for you.
First week in the books.

Dec 12 20
I have never heard more unsolicited advice, mostly negative- then when I was pregnant, parenting, or healing cancer.

You want to share encouragement? Let me hear it.

You want to share stories of hope? Let's go!

You want to share a hug, pat on the back or an encouraging smile? Very welcome.

What is not welcome are the comments, and stories of death or looks of pity. Those stories are not about me, or you- friend. If you hear them, I encourage you to kindly ask to them to stop or ask if they have an encouraging story, or walk away!

For new parents, Mamas, I encourage you to do the same, you've got this.
Who knew that both scenarios would prompt such negative projections of people's own fear and insecurities.

Cheers to healing, to fostering a healing mindset that has no room for doubt, no room for other's fears or insecurities.

Jan 22
This whole experience feels so similar to pregnancy and postpartum that I laugh and cry from time to time. The tumor is located in my pelvis and puts pressures on the same muscles and the same attachments that are involved in third trimester pregnancy.

Every morning I say good morning to it and check to see if there have been any changes, skin changes, size, texture, mobility. At night I check it again and pray that it will be time for it to leave my body. The same as I did when I was pregnant with my girls.

Sitting down on the toilet hurts during really bad moments, to the point where Danny helps me— as he did postpartum.

Sitting isn't the same, I have to adjust based on discomfort and can't sit for too long, and can't stand for too long. And sleeping? Can't sleep on my belly anymore. It's a mix of feeling pregnant and postpartum.

The only difference is this time we won't have a baby in our arms. I'll be rebirthed through this whole process, as will Danny as we navigate this whole thing.

Could this be one of our greatest blessings

| 9 |

It Tore Through Her Skin

When it was clear that we were losing ground with this second fast growing tumor, we discussed treatment changes with our oncologist. This was a heartbreaking moment. It had been about seven months since her surgery; there was pain every day, sleepless nights, and four weeks confined to bed with an open, draining tumor wound. We are much past inconvenience and frustration. The journey turned again.

The lima bean sized lymph node on her left hip had grown to the size of a large grapefruit. It was absolutely terrifying. We had been getting treatments at an integrative care center, but it was clear the tumor was out of control. The pain was unbearable. On Thanksgiving we went to the emergency room because the tumor had come to the surface of her skin and looked like it was going to burst. It was located on her front side where her thigh met her torso, the inguinal crease.

Thank You, Cancer

Imagine having a grapefruit stuck under your skin there. When the ER staff learned she had a cancer history, they denied us any care; just gave her an expensive workup and some pain meds. What a joke. We continued to monitor the site as the tumor literally grew moment by moment, exponentially until her skin eventually pulled apart. The tumor tore through her skin. It's easy to just glance over those words.

Tore. Through. Her. Skin.

After the tumor burst through her skin and drained, it left a half-dollar-sized hole that remained for over a year. Put the tip of your index finger to the tip of your thumb. That was the size of the hole. Through it oozed tissue and fluid of all colors. We went through truckloads of gauze. Truckloads might be an understatement to be honest. The horror was real. I saw it, and couldn't unsee it. I didn't feel it; but she felt every bit. Her tolerance for pain seemed otherworldly. Incredibly, she managed to still be present as a wife and mother. She still smiled and laughed and read to the girls. This is far beyond any strength I have ever witnessed.

I came across this picture from months ago and paused to read the shirt. "Fight like a Mother" has never felt so true and I have never

felt the depth of those words, as I do now.

Our dear friend @gigiyogini has started a gofundme page to ease our stress at this moment in our lives. We don't know how long this journey is going to be. We don't know what tonight will even look like. Danny has taken on more responsibility to support us financially as well as in the home as l am off my feet more frequently. Many have asked how they can help and support us while so many of you are miles away and well, things are strange in the world right now.

If you are able and feel pulled to contribute to this journey and all it entails, please do.

This journey has felt far less lonely these past couple of weeks as we have chosen to share the journey rather than carry the burden alone. Thank you. Thank you for the unwavering love for myself and my family.

After that Thanksgiving trip to the ER, our provider steered us to a cancer center in Tulsa, OK, the Cancer Treatment Center of America or CTCA. We had a few options for providers. We knew well the challenges of being treated locally. The convenience of being home every night was an all too familiar fallacy we had come to know so well. For months we had been going to treatment every day in town and it took its toll. The time in the car, the back and forth, the time off work, the care for our girls, etc. No one was able to get much rest, and most importantly Raff wasn't able to get the healing time that she needed.

In Tulsa at the CTCA consult, they told us Raff would need chemo, radiation, and she would need to be there five days a week for nine weeks. We had to think hard about that. We lived more than three hours from Tulsa, we had the two girls, and I worked full time. HOW? Oh yeah, and the cost. There was the whole money hurdle as well. We're talking hundreds of thousands of dollars of treatment. We have like $27 to our name. Insurance might cover it. HUH?

It was in this decision-making process that an entirely new aspect of marriage emerged for us. I was 100% fully in with the chemo and radiation move. I was done watching Raff suffer and done with all the pain she was dealing with. I was in. She was not. God bless her, and her fight, and her wild spirit. She did not want to do it. Or at least she was so conflicted that she wasn't willing to budge. Keep in mind she has this open, leaking tumor that tore through her flesh; yet, she still sat here on the living room floor and was resistant. She wasn't going to do it. I was livid. I was so angry.

But I learned a very important lesson in those moments. I committed to her. I loved her. Our marriage was one of teamwork and grace, and honoring each other. Regardless of my thoughts, this was her choice. I had an opinion of course and was entitled to it, but the choice was hers. I chose to hold space for her. I chose to walk with her. I chose to support her. I laid down my sword and chose to unite. She eventually chose treatment, but that was not the only important part of this moment. It was paramount that we went about this decision as a team. It was important that she felt supported. It was important that we were all in. It was important that we were on the same side of the table. There was no room for doubt or disagreement or angst between the two of us. We sat in the proverbial mud together and worked it out. Our marriage grew to new heights in those moments, and it was very much needed as you will find out in the coming chapters. I learned a very important distinction between men and women then. As men, we want the solution; women are concerned with working together. I needed constant reminders because otherwise we were speaking different languages.

The CTCA provided conventional options, as well as holistic support, counseling, rehabilitation, a hotel, cafe, and hospital all in the same building. The convenience was amazing, the people were far above. Everyone had such a passion for their work. From doctors, to maintenance staff, to nurses, hotel staff, and drivers. They were incredible, and I couldn't imagine pursuing treatment any other way. When we went there, we were introduced to the team over the course of a week. They formulated a treatment plan, we met with three doctors, had a

It Tore Through Her Skin

PET scan and two blood panels, met with three counselors, an educator, a pastor, had two 4-hour infusions for high calcium levels and an MRI. We came back the next week for another very productive week of appointments, too. This was all done at a mindblowing pace, and all of the doctors and nurses were behind the scenes constantly coordinating care and speaking to each other. I would imagine this amount of activity would have taken more than six months elsewhere, and at this point, time was of the essence. So we were very thankful for their efficiency.

Since deciding to move forward with treatment in Tulsa it was clear Raff would have to live there for nine weeks. But, our family didn't do apart; we did everything together. Cancer aside, being away from her girls for nine weeks might take her out. There had to be a way.

I stayed the first weeks in Tulsa with Raff to help get everything started and the girls stayed with my parents. Some close friends helped out as well. We were so thankful to everyone who stepped up to help with our children in our absence. As the weeks stretched out, I picked up Raff every Friday in Tulsa, drove home, then we drove back to CTCA on Sundays. This was an eight-hour round trip on Fridays, and then another eight-hour round trip on Sundays. Family and friends went to Tulsa and stayed with Raff a week at a time to give her some lifesaving company.

| 10 |

Parkour!

That time gave us an unanticipated gift. Raff had one-on-one time with her mom, step-mom, brother, sister, a lifelong friend, and with me. Our trips to Tulsa became dates. At least we would treat them as such. Come to think of it, all of these doctors appointments all those years, we considered dates. Coffee on the front end, or after, and some laughs on the way. I'll never forget when she walked with a cane, she slowly, barely inched her way up onto a curb, and she exclaimed, "Parkour!" We laughed so hard. For those who don't know, parkour is a sport in which extreme athleticism is required to move about obstacles that require running, jumping, etc. Humor was a way that we connected and honored our love inside of this horror-filled reality. If we set aside the reason, all that time was really a gift; and it was in this season that we began to see another side of cancer.

It goes without saying that the logistics of treatment in another city was not our only hurdle. The other looming issue was the financial piece, the cost of treatment. How could we manage it? We had many angels surrounding us throughout this whole journey. We hadn't thought of them as angels before; they were friends, family, acquaintances, even strangers. But now with Raff's life on the line and our backs against the wall, when they delivered just what we needed at just the right time, what else were they but angels?

Our friend Gigi was one. She created a GoFundMe to help with this massive financial commitment to the CTCA. We knew from the start we were many tens of thousands of dollars in the hole, so every move was so stressful. I remember the moment in our kitchen when the GoFundMe took off. Raff had always existed in a moment all her own. She wasn't aware of the time, she didn't care about social media, she couldn't care less about the news, she was always IN THE MOMENT, something I will always cherish, because I learned from the best. I had my phone in my hand and checked the GoFundMe which was posted the day before. Unbelievably, it had topped $50,000. Our path was now possible! I showed Raff and she was overcome with a deluge of emotion. She always had the hardest time accepting love; a hurdle we struggled to surmount in our early days. In this moment the love was strikingly obvious; she felt it, and the relief that burst forth from her was nothing short of amazing. It broke through to her in a way this pittance of words could never convey. I still feel it in my heart.

Through it all, our love was rampant. It was wild and free. It moved outside of schedules and distance and family. It was the conqueror, and it held us all together.

I could not talk about the team we had without telling you about God's role. Never once did I doubt that God walked us down this path. But there were countless moments that He showed Himself to us to reinforce our belief in Him. Broken was how we felt so many times. We tried and tried and tried, and our efforts didn't land. Things didn't make sense. Pain wouldn't cease.

She had a real broken moment on her first day of chemo and radiation.

She was really feeling beat down, and fear was closing in. I was feeling that way too. As I remember, we had just received the news that Raff would be starting those dreaded conventional treatments. Neither of us was looking forward to them. We ended up here on the back of the massive and erratic growth of this tumor. Pain brought us here. Fear brought us here. Love held us together. Hope kept breath in our lungs, and each step seemingly lit up as we stepped into it. It would soon be wildly clear just who had the flashlight.

We were heading back up to our room to emotionally break down after very heavy meetings with some doctors. Her first treatments would begin that afternoon, and all of this was quite overwhelming. I pushed her wheelchair into the elevator and just before the doors closed this upbeat couple snuck in. Our mood was terrible. I had that protective husband vibe going and wasn't wanting anyone ruffling our feathers. We were both scared, we were both heartbroken, and we were both teary eyed. Despite our defensive body language and averted eyes, the man was undeterred. He said, "How y'all doin?" in the most cheerful voice. I so badly wanted to tell him off, end him, protect our space, really anything but talk. But something about this man lowered our defenses. We briefly explained our plight, and he immediately asked, "Do you know the difference between the people that make it here, and the ones that don't?" We shook our heads. "The ones that have a relationship with Jesus. Those are the ones that make it. The others, well I don't know about them." His message was clear as day. The elevator opened, and as they slipped out the man turned and said, "Don't think that I was on this elevator by accident." The man and his lady went about their day, all smiles. We were silent. Lost in our thoughts. Did we just meet Jesus on the elevator? It sure felt that way.

"Therefore everyone who hears these words of mine and puts them into practice is like a wise man who built his house on the rock. The rain came down, the streams rose, and the winds blew and beat against that house; yet it did not fall, because it had its foundation on the rock. But everyone who hears these words of mine and does not put them into practice is like a foolish man who built his house on sand. The rain came down, the streams rose, and the winds blew and beat against that house, and it fell with a great crash." Matthew 7:24-27

Up to this point, we hadn't talked too much about Jesus, but we had both definitely been praying more than daily. There were also tons and tons of people reaching out telling us they were praying, too; so there was no doubt it could have been a divine appointment in that elevator. I can't say everything was instantly better, or our tears stopped, because more definitely came. Floods and floods of tears. But also, we felt some relief. Just as when the random lady in the parking lot said, "Jesus is with you." Relief. The fear subsided a bit, and a new fortitude seemed to rise within us. Suddenly taking the next step seemed more possible. And we did, we went to her appointments and the rest was just easier to bear.

"And, you are helping us by praying for us. Then many people will give thanks because God has graciously answered so many prayers for our safety." 2 Corinthians 1:11 [NLT]

We continued on to treatment emboldened by the reminder that our team was much more powerful than we could imagine. When we realized that we were not in control, it was an important crossroad in our life. It was also a tremendous opportunity for us to rely on something outside ourselves. Our prayer game had been on point, and without a doubt we felt the momentum of all the prayers on our behalf. We were so grateful to everyone, mostly to the Big Man upstairs.

Quick note: Life had overwhelming simplicity and clarity back then. I think it truly can be that way in our daily lives, but we have managed to cloud them up quite proficiently. I hope that reading this story steers all of us into living in such a way that we place value on that which is really irreplaceable, our health and our time together. Much love to you.

| 11 |

Blessed By Cancer

This was the end of WEEK 1. Five radiation treatments, one round of chemo.

You get a schedule at the Center when you walk in that tells you what your week will look like. Then, you walk over to this rollercoaster, and its as big as the center- winding around going up and down and then zig-zag— each of the curves and turns is an emotion - like anger then you go up in the ride and feel hope then it takes a hard right and you feel sadness then wait— eerrrrr to the left you feel relief and you just ride the rollercoaster all week and get off when you have appointments. It's the craziest shit I've ever experienced.

JK no rollercoaster, just cancer.

Thank You, Cancer

Feb 21 21

When they talk about cancer they don't tell you about all the opportunities it will bring. Don't get me wrong, I'm not sitting here ecstatic that I'm in treatment for cancer. What I am ecstatic about and so deeply grateful for, which I never expected— is the time I've had with my family.

At first we freaked out a bit thinking about all the weeks that I would need a caregiver with me. It was decided early on that Danny would not be my sole caregiver through this, that he would be home with the girls so they would have one parent with them through the variables of this journey.

Now, looking back at each week and finishing my sixth week of treatments, as I say good-bye to my mother as we go our separate ways. I would have never had time with each of my siblings, family friend, and mothers in my life-without kids, for FIVE whole days— ever. We all have our children, jobs, lives; but this whole cancer thing opened up time to laugh about spilled olives, crying on shoulders, and sharing a fuck yeah I completed another week.

I wouldn't wish this on anyone but it's not all bad news, heartbreak, and hair loss. I could cry tears of joy for the time it has created.

I remember the conversations that we had about this time. We were just awestruck at what cancer had given us. The outpouring of support, the time with our family and friends. It was just tremendous, we felt so blessed. One day we were reminiscing about the weeks she was in Tulsa and she said something I never could have imagined hearing in the same phrase.

Thank You, Cancer.

| 12 |

Unwelcome Adjustments

I remember the morning I watched four-year-old Ace cry on FaceTime with Mama. I sat next to her and cried too. There were moments that struck us so deep, moments that pierced to the core. That one got me. I don't routinely gush with emotion, but I was free flowing. Five-year-old Rue has always had this deep connection to others. She sees and feels everything. She saw my tears that morning and came over and sat on my lap. She was saving me with everything her big beautiful soul had. Those days life was different: Mama was off during the week getting the treatment she so desperately needed, the three of us were home trying to hold on to the normalcy we were accustomed to, then we were reunited as a unit on the weekends. How sweet the weekends were! Never long enough though.

As the weeks rolled on we tried to get into a routine, all the while knowing that our life was in such turmoil. The gap was felt by all of us. We all dealt with it in different ways. There was definitely not a wrong set of feelings or emotions, but we never let those emotions create distance between us. We were strong, because we were together. The strength of our family was the unit.

It was after work one evening when I stopped to pick up the girls at my parents' house. We had dinner there and as we were leaving Rue had an out-of-control meltdown. I will spare the details, but it turned into a freak out that lasted about 25 minutes. Unconsolable. My heart broke for her. By the time she calmed down, we were all totally spent. I don't recall the issue, but whatever it was, it wasn't really the issue. It was abundantly clear that she was just struggling in general. Thankfully it ended with a loving Papa-Rue embrace. I thanked the Lord for those moments when we could work through the pain.

As adults, we found some solace in routine, some calm in the sameness of activity. Was this a mistake? An oversight that naively allowed us to continue this pattern of craziness. Change was constant. Not surprising. But if our connection was consistent, even though it was a challenge, it brought us through. Our connection, our relationships, our investment in our people carried us when we lost sight of ourselves or our sanity. This time was confusing for us as adults. Hell, imagine being a kid!

Here's what I have. Being present in your day, being present with your family, being available in the moment is everything.

Exist now.

Own yourself now.

Love now.

Invest in now.

On my second week of chemotherapy and radiation I woke up from being passed out from the premeds they administer to a

phone call that I needed a blood transfusion.

A WHAT?!?! Stop. Thats not real. I havent lost blood.

I soon learned that my blood count had dropped to the point where they would have to stop treatment if I didnt agree to it. I STRUGGLED with it, honestly- I always said that I would only get a blood transfusion in case of an emergency, and then the reality hit that cancer is an emergency. I agreed to the blood transfusion and two liters later (thank God for blood donors) and after the pre-meds wore off, I felt like a million bucks. No joke, felt like I could run a marathon and could not sleep!

Last week was a second blood transfusion. One liter, and I was up LATE and full of energy and felt like I was hung over the next morning.

No one talks about the details. I didnt know blood transfusions were a part of the cancer, chemo, radiation journey. I never expected blood transfusions to get me through.

| 13 |

She Danced

It was on a Saturday. The night before we had come home from the treatment center. Three weeks of treatment down and over half way. Huge victory! She has been gone all week, and she was home for the weekend.

In the excitement to get home Friday night we had a good laugh. Apparently I couldn't stop talking and Raff basically told me to shut up because she needed to sleep. Hilarity in the midst of tiredness. Our banter hadn't stopped, and it was so refreshing.

The dance of parenting little ones during this season was chaotic. The weekly reunions were so charged. They were HUGE! There were so many feelings present and so much obvious exhaustion in all of us. I even took a nap that Saturday, and I can count on one hand my naps as an adult. Each of the girls had their own expression of the storm of feelings going on inside. Some days it was all I could do to just keep it together.

We so wanted to enjoy those weekends together, and music became a big part of the routine. Our refuge. Raff and I had always loved music. It was an aspect of our relationship that always rings true, and brings us right into harmony. There are a litany of songs that will make us cry instantly, in the best of ways of course. Rue used to dance in Raff's belly to the bass hits in *Baby Got Back*. Chris Stapleton has so many songs that rile all of us up. So that Saturday night we fired up the tunes. We had a speaker that lights up like a dance party and the girls LOVE IT! As we cruised down the list, singing at the top of our lungs in the dark with disco lights going, something happened that filled me with joy.

She danced! Raff stood up and danced with the girls. My eyes are full of tears writing this. That may not seem like much to you, but for us, it was HUGE! She spent six weeks in bed before treatment. If you do the math, that was ten weeks in pain, exhaustion, and very limited mobility. But, that night she danced! If there were a short list of expressions of who Raff was at the center of her soul, dancing would be on there. And that night she danced! It was like a fountain of life poured forth from her. These were the moments we held on to. The next day she was sore and tired. I guess it was to be expected after the glory of the night before and her lack of movement for such a long period of time.

As treatment carried on, it would be easy to just begin to fade. It would be easy to begin losing who she was, and what made her. There were so many obstacles, and so many chances to give up; what was of utmost importance was to hold on to the fiber of who she was and the things that made her shine. I hadn't been in her shoes, but I was right next to her this whole way and saw the darkness. It was terrifying. On the contrary, it had no comparison to the light within her. There was always the choice. I can't help but draw the parallel for all of us as we decide who we will be each day. We almost always have the ability to make the choice that is truer to ourselves. Or, on the flip side, the choice that leads to us fading. That really got me thinking.

It was my observation that this serious health issue brought everything to the present. The 10,000 foot view seemed almost irrelevant as each day, heck, each moment carried the weight of the world. It made us carefully consider our choices, our values, our people, and our time. Fluff just fell away, and the BS of daily life seemed so silly. In these moments the core of our being seemed to be called into question. And, I see how this has relevance for all of us. What are the things in your life that make you? Who are you at your core? Let all fall away, and what is left? I encourage you to sit in thoughtful silence. Because in these moments of surrender, I believe you find what sets you free. It was terrifying to admit we don't have control. It was terrifying to realize this ride may actually be over tomorrow, or today for that matter. Taking the moments, or days, or weeks, or years to disassemble the armor of life that we unknowingly take on and find what lies within, may just be the key that unlocks the gate to fulfillment, simple acceptance, and/or self love.

This health crisis we had cast light on so much. It created so much love and connection in our world from all of you. It distilled our values down to the simple things that make this life rich. As we looked forward, our path was the one we were meant to be on. It was the one we were most equipped for. My hope for you is that you focus on that which brings you light as well. Focus on the best within you. If you have one day, or you have 100 years, let your soul shine. That weekend I saw Raff's soul shine, and that gave me great hope.

| 14 |

Behind the Curtain

Tomorrow is my LAST day of chemotherapy.

Tomorrow I will get my pre-meds, get chemo, they will take out my PICC line in my arm (the tube they use to give me meds and take blood), and then a beautiful melody of voices (no pressure, nurses) will sing me a good-bye chemotherapy song.

I've been alone for the past few days reflecting on this journey and it doesnt seem quite real. But having a song sung to me and my PICC line removed and Danny there to celebrate with me!?! Make out session!!! JK JK
It's getting real that I get to go home soon and heal for surgery. Oh, and only T H RE E more radiation treatments.

Mar 24 21
There were seven weeks where I was at Cancer Treatment Centers

of America. In those seven weeks, I attended over 100 appointments with varying doctors, specialists, surgeons, and therapists. At the time I was in an emergency situation.

When I got home I felt the need to continue the constant appointments because I still had the feeling that healing was in other people's hands, as well as mine. I felt so lost at this in between stage of healing and waiting. There was time for rest too but I was overstimulated, over scheduled and overwhelmed by so much.

Once I decided to take a break from so many appointments, and lean into my own power of healing.

The healing power of REST. Woooooooo it has taken my healing to a peaceful place. It's not about other people and their schedules. It's about me.

Your healing is about YOU.
If you are tired, rest.

Too many appointments? Schedule them differently, schedule life on YOUR terms. It's scary to get quiet and pull back in a world that tells you the answer is everywhere BUT within. When you do find that moment where you make the decision to do life on YOUR healing time, oweeee it feels good. The tension begins to dissolve, the anxiety begins to dissolve, you find a new resting place.

Cheers to believing in the power of rest and YOUR ability to heal.

When I first read about radiation and the process of beginning radiation in cancer treatment- I read about the tattoos.
That little black dot a couple centimeters under my belly button is one of a few tattoos I was given to mark my body with the purpose of precision in administering radiation treatment to the right places and not burn the rest of me.
When I first read about them, I thought "What the fuck?!" When

the radio geologist gave me my dots I still thought "WTF, man."

Before each of the radiation treatments I made sure that the nurses saw them and that we lined my body up exactly right before rolling into the machine.

As time went on, I became so grateful for these little black dots around my pelvis because the purpose of precision was saving organ function and limiting pain, discomfort and unnecessary damage.

When I first got home from treatment, I felt sadness everytime I looked at them.

Yesterday, as I lifted up my shirt to get some sunshine on this belly of mine- I felt love to an old friend. A nod of, I see you, we did it.

The girls ask about them sometimes and I tell them they're my love dots the doctor gave me to make sure the picture was just right.

As time and space increase between challenging experiences in your past, and the present— the perspectives and emotions around the situation change.

The marking hasn't really changed but everything else has changed 100X over. I have made peace with so much, the scars, the scar tissue, seen and unseen.

It's nice... it's nice not to hate the process anymore.

A healing hang-over from yesterday.

Thank You, Cancer

I used to get frustrated at the ups and downs of this whole wild ride of healing cancer. Now I get it. The rest the body needs even after a joy filled day. It's not bad— it's actually great, not in fight or flight, not in a survival mentality, of I have to "fight" or "kill" or whatever aggressive terminology that sends the opposite message of safety to a body that so deeply requires safety and removal of that survival response. I've always hated those words when it came to cancer.

So today, after a night of feeling the need to feast until the early hours of the morning— we played, we laughed, we drew, we played and I napped and then napped again, bath and breathwork and bed. Some days it just looks like that.

As the reality has crashed into me, that stage 4 cancer doesn't just disappear - these weeks of being thrown back into an intensity of tumors, research and hard conversations— I have decided to share more openly about my/our journey.
When I was diagnosed three years ago, there wasn't much information out there. As I dive back into the World Wide Web, the resources out there are growing, but minimal. For us young mothers, young women, diagnosed with cancer or other severe autoimmune illnesses the resources can feel incredibly daunting and depressing.

If this whole crazy journey, that has encompasses multiple therapies of conventional medicine as well as "alternative" methods can bring hope or some comfort to another- I'm happy to share.

As I share I have one request.

My hope is that you do not view me as a sick person but a person dealing with sickness who is healing. That as I openly share the parts that are vulnerable especially due to the location of the cancer- that I am still me. That you see ME and that you don't see the exposed cancer first.

I realize I have not shared as much because of the location of the tumors and how so much is layered in the conversation of my diagnosis, a woman's sacred body and so much more. The layers that keep peeling away.

May this story, our story and experience of heartbreak but also pure JOY, community, love, deep deep healing, parenting through chronic illness, marriage in the face of a heavy diagnosis, freedom in acceptance, the reality of a cancer diagnosis in America—may all these topics and conversations bring light.

Thank you all for the support these years
you the realest.

There is a lot of talk about the immune system, but not on the lymphatic system. One of our greatest weapons against infection that gets little attention is the system of highways that run alongside the circulatory system and the organs that it encompasses-making up the immune system. The circulatory system has a pump called the heart but the lymphatic system does not have a pump.

The lymphatic system relies on muscle contractions and other functions of the body to pump the fluid and clean up carbon dioxide, fats, proteins, and pathogens. One of the functions it relies on is BREATH.

When we breathe deeply, our lymphatic system is assisted in pumping and dumping into the thoracic duct which then dumps the filtered fluid back into the bloodstream. When the lymphatic system does not get pumped, it becomes stagnant. All the gunk and pathogens that the lymphatic system filters out, gets clogged creating a growing list of ailments and issues in the body. As a cancer patient or person living with chronic illness, it is IMPERATIVE to keep the lymphatic system moving to prevent stickiness, metastasis, assist in detoxing and prevent lymphedema.

We may not always be able to walk, exercise or move our bodies as we would like due to illness, postpartum, c-section, surgery, flights, work...BUT we can always BREATHE. Deep belly breaths, pump the lymphatic system even when we can't do backflips and star jumps. Put your hands on your belly and get to breathing, baby.

Prior to lymphatic massage, I could not walk standing up straight. The tumor had grown too large, the skin, muscles, fascia and nerves had stretched too far to be comfortable in any way. I walked holding onto a wheelchair or I sat in the wheelchair and had a caretaker push me.

After my first consult with the radiologist, she immediately sent me over to physical therapy where I received my first lymphatic massage.

I kid you not, I got up from the table and walked standing up STRAIGHT to the wheelchair to push it on my own, standing up!!

From that massage, I immediately felt that I had to study the lymphatic system and do everything I could to help myself. I hope to break down the information I have learned into very small, digestible pieces for you. It's not complicated, it's not expensive, it is massively important.

I urge you, if you are healing from chronic illness, healing cancer, or want to prevent illness, lymphatic massage and movement should be a part of your world.

Your hands are healing, rub them gently on your skin towards your heart and show your lymph's some love.
If you feel you may need professional help, please find a medical provider to assist you.

| 15 |

Nipples out of Nothing

Part 1: Nipples out of nothing
As the elevator doors opened and I wheeled myself out, the plastic surgeon's nurse exclaimed, "I'm so happy for you! You have a consult with Dr. P! She can make nipples out of nothing!"

"Well that's great news! Maybe she can do a little something for me while she's down there!" By down there I mean my pelvis. My left inguinal area where the radiation and chemo were successful and melted the tumor, along with my skin away. Where the radiation burnt and shrunk other parts as well.

Days later Danny and I walked into the office with both plastic surgeons quiet and focused. With permission, they measure the wound, grab onto my thighs, grab onto my stomach and back, they feel the muscles and continue to measure. At 120lb and 5'8 there isn't much to pull from, I watch them try to find a patch large enough, thick enough.

"She can make nipples out of nothing." I repeat in my mind.

"Nipples out of nothing. She can do this." I whisper to myself. Danny watches from the bench against the wall as both surgeons and the nurse hover over me.

"We're going to have to cut an 8" x 11" to get all the radiated tissue and clean margins. Then Dr. P will take grafts from your thighs, stomach or back to cover the area."— as they speak my eyes look over my body. The size of the area they would remove, the sections of my body they would remove and then re-place. My brain clues back into the conversation, "We may have to separate the surgeries into two different ones depending how you do."

"Can we take pictures?" I stand up with Danny's help and hold up my top, and my robe. I turn and wait "click", "turn another 45 degrees.
"Click"
We thanked the surgeons after they encouraged us, assured us that though it was a complex surgery, it wasn't the hardest one they had ever completed as they referred to reconstructing chest cavities. They had faith my body would recover. It would be a long recovery but I would recover.

"Focus on recovering and healing, right now"

We walked out of the office, oddly at peace though I just heard how my body would be cut up and put back together.
"She can make nipples out of nothing." I whispered to myself.

On March 29th, 2021 I was sent home from the Treatment Center in Tulsa. It had been about nine weeks back and forth between Kansas and Oklahoma for appointments. Thirty five treatments of radiation, seven rounds of chemo, and approximately 110 appointments in between- blood draws, blood transfusions, lymphatic massage, oncologists, radiologist, therapists. My A-team in Tulsa to my A-team in Kansas which looked a little different, Danny, my children and every single person that kept life steady and as consistent as possible for my children, the outpouring of love from friends and family-my A++ team.

After some time being home and adjusting to basically being on an island and then getting thrown into the real world (on that in a different post), I received a text message from a friend with the news that the Treatment Center planned on shutting it's doors June 1st. No big deal, I mean "holy shit, what the fuck?" deal but my surgery was scheduled for May 5th so, all good.

A few days passed as Danny and I tried to come up with a game plan to move forward in finding a new oncologist and hopes of another group of champs to support us through this very long roller coaster. My phone rang and a number from Broken Arrow, OK popped up.

"Yes! We'll have a plan and schedule for surgery!" I thought.

Part 2 :: Amputate

I pick up the phone anticipating the Center calling to schedule all the details of the surgery. Darren had called me earlier and shared the news that the Center was closing. "There's no way they're going to cancel the surgery though. That's just a few weeks away!"

"Hi!",", expecting to hear the nipples nurse calling to do a run through.
"We have to cancel the surgery, we don't feel it is safe enough in the timeframe to continue with the plan." said a woman I had never heard before.

"What do you mean? Everything is planned..."

After pleading with this woman, getting transferred to other doctors. They assured me they would set up surgical consults at the other Centers. "Okay, we'll try Chicago." My brother is there, we can stay with him, still driving distance if we needed to, it's okay- Chicago.

Danny and I are ushered into an exam room by the nurse, with a robe on the table— I am asked to disrobe completely.

"Not everything right?" | ask the nurse, as I have never had to completely disrobe for my exams.

"Everything off" — I look at Danny flustered and he helps me change into the robe. Three doctors slowly trickle in as the nurse stands against the counter and Danny stays by my side.

"We want to wait at least six months and then we'll re-evaluate."

My jaw drops. I begin to tear up. The questions begin. "That is not what we were told. I was scheduled for surgery...this doesn't make sense…..what do I do with an open wound??" | try to listen as Danny asks questions and the plastic surgeon answers, seemingly annoyed. I ask again, "but what do I do with a gaping wound??" The plastic surgeon is to my right and he exclaims, "we'll do you want an amputated leg?!" I respond between tears, "I'm well aware of the dangers, that's not helpful." Danny chimes in, "You haven't even looked at her. You haven't even looked at the area." Up until that point, the surgeons and oncologist were standing against the wall, the plastic surgeon putzing around with his ego in tow.

They ask to see the wound and continue with their stance that they will not do surgery. lask, "So what happens?" The oncologist against the wall near the door, the last to walk in, the one who admittedly did not see my records— with the least information and greatest opinion speaks up. "You'll go home, heal from radiation the cancer will continue to come back and then hospice."

Nipples out of Nothing

I begin to weep and beg Danny to take me home. Danny begins to speak protective words to the man so cold, so inhumane, as he works to find my clothes. To my right the nurse walks over in tears, crying over me as she helps Danny get all my clothes back onto my delicate healing body.

Then I notice the quiet one. The quiet doctor in the corner that only gently spoke a few words. He had no eyebrows and no hair on his head. I know that not all baldness is due to chemotherapy but was he quiet because he knew. He knew, because he knows.

We walk out of the twilight zone and into my brother's car. In awe and absolute despair and disgust.

We have taken multiple trips to find a team within the network that we felt would be the best fit. We found a great team in Georgia.

Our next stop was the CTCA in Atlanta, GA, to see a reconstructive surgeon, Dr. Durden.

Part 3 :: Durden

"What?? What doctors?... I'm going to make some calls.

Let's get you to Georgia." Exclaimed my previous radiologist.

We packed our bags again. Hopped on a flight to GA and was welcomed by a shuttle sent by the Center. We arrived at the hotel tired but hopeful, I mean how much worse could it get?

We walked into the exam room, where I DID NOT disrobe completely. I put the pink robe on, assuming it was pink because of all the reconstructive breast surgery due to breast cancer. I looked at the implant on the counter and waited nervously.

The plastic surgeon's PA showed up asking some questions and we talked about radiation burns. We discussed the process of healing burns and he showed his own healing on his calf that was clearly very painful. His own story, disarming my nervousness. The appointment was already waaaay better than Chicago's.

Then he walked in.

Walked straight over to introduce himself with a kind but firm handshake. He sat down in the chair right in front of me. He asked for me to talk to him about what was going on. I began to explain— and then over explain- and then passively ask for what I wanted —- then over explained again. Then he stopped me.

"You want me to call your radiologist? Tell me what you want. You don't have to explain." In that moment, awe. Really? I didn't HAVE to explain? I didn't HAVE to feel less than or that I didn't know what I was talking about so l over explained in hopes of being seen as an intelligent, educated, patient?

Wait, I didn't have to explain?

Being human, sitting across from another human was enough for my wants and needs to be heard? Dayum.
"I'll call her! Let's look and see what's going on." He waited for me to lift my robe and cover my body the way I felt most comfortable. With consent, he assessed. "There's not much to take from. The best thing would be to create a flap from your abdomen but I don't want to do that to you. You're young, with these beautiful abs."

"I even get a complement during an assessment? Whoa." I thought to myself.

"I really think it will heal on its own." He stated after completing his assessment.

Danny and I looked at each other and chuckle/ choke. Ha! No.

"This is going to heal on it's own? How? What about infection?"

I stare into the crater the size of grapefruit that the tumor left in my groin. The crater that posed a threat literally so deep, sepsis could take me out.

The difference between the denial of this appointment and the last? The denial of the surgery wasn't due to fear of amputation. It wasn't filled with fear inducing comments of hospice. It wasn't filled with disrespect to the human or the human spirit that navigates cancer. It was filled with hope. It was filled with faith in MY body and respect to the capacity of the body in general. It was filled with the belief in miracles.

The visit with the reconstructive surgeon was so relaxed. Dr. Durden had a wonderful, gentle bedside manner and his communication skills were excellent. He was so chill. He seemed as relaxed as a man grilling at a weekend barbeque. Raff nervously stuttered a bit during their conversation and he just calmly asked her what she wanted. He wasn't there to push some agenda on us. He was actually there for her. We were so taken aback we could have both cried, and we probably did. He took a look at her hip, and he thought about his answer for a bit. He said, "I think it will heal, let's just leave it alone." Raff and I both laughed thinking, *Yeah right. Are you looking at the same hole we are? You could put a tennis ball in there.* But, he held the line. He said, "Let's just check back in three months and we'll go from there."

We had so many doubts and emotions. As positive as we felt about our encounter with Dr. Durden, we were disappointed. Our hearts and minds were set on surgery. It had to happen. Our hopes had been dashed back when the Tulsa CTCA cancelled our surgery, then we were turned away and discouraged in Chicago, now this Atlanta surgeon said to wait three months. In our minds, we couldn't even wait three more days!

But in time, unbelievable as it sounds, that hip healed. That tennis-ball-sized crater healed over! We thought it was impossible. We were devastated that the center in Tulsa closed because, in our minds, Raff had to have the surgery there. We couldn't see it then, but looking back, we could see it was His plan. The center closed and Raff was spared from an unneeded surgery. He synced up the timelines. Incredible.

"He controls the course of world events; he removes kings and sets up other kings, He gives wisdom to the wise, and knowledge to the scholars." Daniel 2:21

We left with an appointment to see Durden soon, easily dressed with Danny's help as we looked at each other in awe. Awe and hope.

I walked into Durden's office months later with a single surgery to remove necrotic tissue, behind us.
He asked to see the area and I proudly exposed the wound.

The HEALING wound.
Durden in awe exclaimed, "I am so happy for you!"

I responded with a huge thank you for filling us with faith rather than fear those months ago.
He responded, "I didn't do anything, that was God, this is all God." He gave me a handshake into a big hug and he expressed his joy for me, again.

I never needed the reconstructive surgery that we were so attached to. I didn't believe my body could heal. I didn't need the authority of the plastic surgeons— but in a way, I did. That's hard to admit, but in the moment with so much trauma to my body. I didn't believe in my body.

I am SO grateful the Center called and my surgery was cancelled.
I am SO grateful that I experienced such distaste in Chicago.

I am SO grateful that the third plastic surgeon— saw my body's ability to heal rather than the opportunity to cut and repair with his own hands.

The area is THICK with scar tissue, discolored, and has a depth to it. It is STILL healing, in all it's beauty and the constant reminder that my body CAN and WILL heal, and my healing is not up to the "authority" of plastic surgeons or any other doctor.

We've got a lot of learning to do about one another; me and these doctors and nurses and therapists and people, more people. It has been two months and counting since my treatment program in Tulsa ended. My heart, body and mind are still healing while also working to find care and get approved for surgery. We have had some pushback (another time for that) which at the time was confusing but as I sit here thinking of ways to mend my soul and make sure I don't completely lose myself in this process of tests, healing, programs, diets and more tests- I realize I needed time. From May 5th to now, I have gone from walking very short distances and laying in bed most days between treatments to walking, 5 squats, gaining strength, and infusing myself and my family with wholeness that we missed while away.

| 16 |

He Held Her Head

So, here we are. Landed in rainy GA for more tests and more updates. Nervous and excited to reach the next checkpoint and to show off my walking without a wheel chair.

Here. We. Are.

Confession: Being home is not what I expected. I would say I wrestle like hard core wrestle on the gym floor with my ear protectors, mouth guard and stylish bodysuit on type of wrestle with deep frustration and gratitude.

Today is one of those wrestling days. Cue the therapist, a lot of tea and a hat over my head and I feel leveled.
When you're in the thick of the fight, of emergency mode healing, there's not much time to process feelings. Face to face with my children, my husband and the day to day, it bubbles over. Every-

thing I've missed, things I'm only kind of taking part in, relationships that have dwindled because I havent been able to physically show up.
The wrestle is real.

During our years with cancer, as our faith grew, He showed up again and again. In turn, Raff and I grew mightily in our faiths. I don't remember the exact moment of this conversation, but will never forget it. Raff was having a rough time with pain at this juncture. During those years, Raff was treated by a lot of different individuals in many healing capacities; many of them were in the most literal sense angels walking among us. She came back from one of those healing sessions one day and told me a story.

"I felt His presence so strong. His strength and tenderness as I felt Him by my head. His hand under my cheek as he whispered to release the shame I carried for it is His to bear, not mine. I broke down in tears weeping forcefully with relief that someone, He was witness- could acknowledge the pain I shouldered as sexual shame ran through my body to parts so sacred that it seeped out of me.

I laid on the ground with each daughter under each armpit snuggled up with my arms open wide against the bed.
Discomfort from radiation burns healing, and that shame still running in my mind. The wheel of shame. Then a stab to my hand and a whisper- I died on the cross for you, let your shame go. I looked at my hand to see if there was a mark from what seemed like a stabbing so real there must be blood. No blood, but the reminder to get off the wheel."

She knew it was Jesus. He was telling her that He had taken away her shame. She actually felt His hands.

"Surely he took up our pain and bore our suffering, yet we considered him punished by God, stricken by him, and afflicted. But he was pierced for our transgressions, he was crushed for our iniquities; the punishment that brought us peace was on him, and by his wounds we are healed. We all, like sheep, have gone astray, each of us has turned to our own way; and the Lord has laid on him the iniquity of us all." Isaiah 53:4-6 [NIV]

She would never make something like that up, she got no bonus points for telling me a story like that. She was always just so connected to life in a transcendent kind of way, more in touch with the spiritual realm than most people. Many times we had experiences with spirits in and out of our home. That was something that was common for us. We'll get to that story; but, for now, when she said Jesus held her head, believe me, He did.

"God is our refuge and strength, an ever-present help in trouble." Psalm 46:1

| 17 |

Gains

This trip is only one night. Man, it should feel so easy, right? Drop in, sleep, appointments, check-ins, wound care and back on a plane home. It should be easier than all the other times, the other trips.

No one told me about all the damage and pain I would feel as a mother, wife, as a woman when biopsies have cleared but the damage to my heart, my body, my soul haven't healed yet.

No one warned me about my child's rage for days anticipating another seperation. We talked about the during, the time away during treatments but no one told me it would become even more painful as they begin to see and feel some togetherness as we get into some sort of routine.

The immediate danger has subsided, with our heads down, and

hearts beholden to the love and support in all corners of our world. No one told me when the fire is out the ashes remain hot to the touch that needs time to settle, and can't be doused with water to tame the heat it continues to produce.

Yet, I sit here watching people walk by boarding planes as I feel so grateful for this body that continues to heal, to the tissue regenerating and knowing my team will feel the same excitement as we stare at this cavity that is filling.
Healing Cancer Journey Update. • A big trip to The Center in Georgia with results from biopsies and surgical consults. Amazing news that there is no sign of cancer in the area where tumor grew. So grateful doctors are on the same page about helping my body heal and not running to surgery.

Thank you to everyone who has encouraged us, sent us their love and support in all sorts of ways. Thank you!

Jul 21

I've done a lot less, "I can't do that." "Not yet." And a lot more "Let's try!" "I can do this today." and
"This feels alright!" even when I'm not sure if I can or should. I'm over all of that limiting talk. The consequences of a little jog can't be worse than the pain I felt not too long ago. The gains and pure joy of a light jog wooooo those consequences, here for it all.

I can do it, I am doing it, and here we are- jogging and surprising myself with a little heel click. A HEEEEEL CLICK BABY! COMIN IN HOT

Less than three months ago, this arm had a PICC line (catheter out your arm) placed in order to receive low dose chemotherapy, blood transfusions and other things.

Gains

This arm now flexes as I make GAINS L so much so that it's catching Danny's attention while I close the car door.

Less than three months ago I was reminded that for every day you lay in bed, it takes about 18 days to gain back strength, mobility and movement.

I'll be flexing over here and dancing in the kitchen as my youngest asks me to dance faster and celebrates how much I can move.

GAINS BABY ALL DAY. (Insert happy tears and happy dance here)

After being diagnosed with cancer over a year ago, I withdrew into a very dark place. I mentally and spiritually struggled, quietly in the evenings or in showers and baths it was my personal hell.

I battled with a fear of death and mostly what I would leave behind for my children. What their life would look like without me, what Danny's life would look like, my siblings and parents— but it always came back to my children. As time went on through treatments and everyday moments, my decisions became about what my children would experience, would they experience a mother who is sick over a toilet constantly, or could we experience a cancer diagnosis in a different way.

When we talk about experience, recall experiences, it reflects the way we feel in that moment. You can be sick in bed with tumors and still experience joy with your loved ones, you can be stranded on the side of the road with a flat tire in the heat but still experience joy and peace.

The emotions you experience in the moment, that's energy - an expression of energy that others can feel around you.

I had to check my stresses and struggles to calm the f*ck down and find some sort of peace. It wasn't helping me, it wasn't helping my children or anyone else around me- but ultimately, it completely blocked my healing and hindered the joy I could feel with my children and the memories we could create.

I have come a long way since my initial diagnosis. I don't panic in the evenings, I don't fear death, and I have tools to regulate my nervous system. What I do keep in the forefront of my mind is that experiences, no matter how painful the situation- reflects the emotions expressed at the time and those emotions are felt as energy. The difference between then and now are the tools in my growing toolkit to regulate my nervous system.

I'll be popping on here more often in the New Year to share what I can to help anyone else who may be struggling.
On August 3rd, 2020 | received my initial diagnosis after a radical vulvectomy to remove a cancerous lesion.
A year later, to the day I am scheduled for another surgery with a very different mindset and body.

Gains

We have these amazing results of negative biopsies which I expected to clear the air and I would feel all sorts of healed - and I do. But the question that keeps showing up for me is "To what level are you WILLING to heal?"
The word healing gets thrown around a lot and it feels heavy for some people as well as light and simple for others.
As I walk into next week and continue on my own very personal path to healing (but like are we ever fully healed? Because life continues to happen? And anything can happen at anytime? Healed for the moment? What does it mean...to me?) ...

I walk into next week as I choose the blade again, in this moment. I ask myself, "What level of healing am I willing to dig into, is my heart ready? How far am I willing to go for the next level of healing?" That blade is not the answer but it is my choice, right now.
leave your judgements of cancer treatments, any and all — at the keyboard in front of you.

| 18 |

Violated and Degraded by TSA

It was 2021 and Raff and I were flying to Atlanta for her treatment. The experience we just had with the TSA in Kansas City was nothing short of degrading, dehumanizing, and shameful. Due to her exposure to chemo and radiation, Raff chose to skip the security scan and opt for a pat down. We had been through security numerous times and despite minor frustrations the pat down worked out.

As usual, before boarding, Raff told the TSA agent that we were going to Atlanta for cancer treatment. She briefly described the tumor; that it was a painful open wound on her groin, it severely limited her movement, but most importantly, it was not to be touched. At that, the agent began the pat down. In spite of Raff's clear instructions though, the agent began touching the tumor. I saw tears well up in Raff's eyes. Again and again, Raff flinched, cringed in pain, and asked the agent to stop. But, undeterred, the agent continued. Traveling was such an uncomfortable stretch for Raff anyway. She didn't need this. I jumped

Thank You, Cancer

in and asked if that was really necessary, reiterating the severity of the wound and the fact that they had been repeatedly asked not to touch it. At that, the agent clearly became uneasy, stopped the pat down, called a manager, and ordered Raff to wait out in front until the manager returned from her break. It was a long 10 minutes that she waited and quietly wept on display for all the travelers who filed past.

The manager finally arrived and we were escorted into a private room. Raff again explained that she was a cancer patient and asked her not to touch the painful open wound. But, same deal. The manager proceeded again with another pat down, and touched the painful tumor wound. Raff began to hyperventilate. The whole ordeal began to seem purposely intrusive, even downright mean. We both had explained, but it fell on deaf ears. Was I supposed to just stand aside in silence and watch someone do this to my wife? God forbid I made too much of a scene about their brazen dehumanizing conduct and risk being removed from the airport or arrested. Both agents should have been ashamed of themselves. And, in no uncertain terms, we told them that.

Raff was already in fear for her life, desperately searching for help, struggling to get to the cancer center who had made the travel reservations. She was not only facing the horror of cancer but she had experienced the horror of past sexual trauma. And to make matters even worse, during all the back and forth with the agents, we heard someone in a loud voice say, "Then don't fly." A snide, ugly, and inexcusable remark, maybe from another employee who had overheard the commotion. As far as I am concerned, that would be grounds for immediate termination. F*cking shameful.

I burned inside as I watched the manager finish and check that her gloves were clean. Of course they were. Then, she simply said, "You're good." And, they all disappeared. They all just walked away. Not even a hint of compassion or empathy. They left Raff. Hyperventilating and sobbing. Just, "You're good." I wanted to say, "You cowards. That was mighty human of you all." I wanted them to feel so much shame from this disgrace.

The screening process needs to be changed. It was monstrous. The TSA agents completely ignored and violated Raff's legitimate requests. No innocent person should be made to feel violated or degraded while traveling. No one should be held hostage by those who were there to protect. But, this was the reality. We couldn't travel unless the TSA had their way with her. I can't imagine what else goes on.

Humiliated and shook, we put her shoes back on and gathered her belongings.

When this whole cancer thing went down I immediately threw myself into reading about radical remission. I threw myself into research and read too many books too quickly for sanity. One book that I started and ended my day with was Radical Remission by Kelly A. Turner. I began to wrestle with miracles, and whether or not I truly believed in them. Beyond hoping for one, but a deep knowing that they happen and even more importantly, that it can happen to me, for me.

I had my faith, but there is a stark difference between hoping and praying and knowing. Being so deep into the faith you have in your body, in the Lord (or who you may or may not pray to), your community around you, that you know it can and will happen.

Some days it was a little bit of desperation clinging onto the knowing when the tumor was growing so fast I could see the difference day to day. It was a "Lord I know you want more for me than this tumor. Lord this is so fucking scary and I recognize that I am only in control of so much but Lord, I know I am on this Earth to do more, to help more."

There were nights I would have to shower to relieve pain and to cover up my cries as I stood there pleading to show me the way, knowing this wasn't going to be it, knowing I was on this Earth for more than just this moment. Those nights I went back to bed and reviewed all the stories of radical remission and healing. I went

through them all in my head over and over as best as I could while coping with the pain.

I now read stories of radical remission, miracles, and healing almost everyday, sometimes multiple times a day.
It has changed my view on life, on tiny moments that go unnoticed.
My heart, my home as become one of miracles.
You could say I'm crazy, kidding myself, whatever- but I know miracles. I wouldn't want to live any other way than having a heart of miracles, a soul of knowing.

How much do you believe in miracles? Do you have a heart of knowing?

| 19 |

Cedric

We had traveled all over during this journey. In the beginning when things started reeling out of control we were just reaching out for anything that seemed like it would work. We called so many doctors, and talked about so many possible routes. We ended up choosing the CTCA on the recommendation of our physician at that time. Little did we know the divine nature of this path. We started out at their center in Tulsa which is where we rode the elevator with Jesus. We spent nine weeks in total there, and the 3.5 hour drive was more or less a commute. After her chemo and radiation, when the Tulsa center closed and surgery was cancelled, we had to trust that the Lord had another path for us. I remember when we received the news that our surgery was dropped from Tulsa's calendar. We were crushed. In shock. Panicked. We had no Plan B. Nothing else. Dig deep and breathe. We just had to trust. Trust that there was something. We had nothing, so we just had to trust that He did. Let go and trust.

We loved the CTCA model of care and knew that they had numerous locations; to us a direct transfer to another location within the CTCA system seemed to make more sense than starting from square one in a new program. Chicago was the next closest to our home, and where Raff's brother and family lived, which would make it a nice two for one. By transferring care to the CTCA in Chicago, we could enjoy family time while there for treatment. Made perfect sense to us. Unfortunately, when we met with those doctors, it was immediately obvious that it was not a good fit. Without going into detail, suffice it to say, it was not even close to a good fit. It was a bad experience. Another door closed.

What now? The CTCA in Atlanta? It would mean air travel which was so hard. Anymore, everything was so hard, but we forced ourselves to at least give it a glance. To our amazement, the Atlanta team was warm, welcoming, and caring. It looked promising. We both were so relieved. We thought we met some new superstars that could help usher in the next chapter in Raff's healing. But, there was more waiting. Waiting for more healing before surgery, and waiting to be accepted for treatment in Atlanta. Weeks passed. It was harder and harder to hold things together while Raff continued to heal from the radiation and chemo. Healing may sound easy, but it wasn't. Plenty of discomfort, lack of sleep, and always new challenges. We were told it could take up to eight weeks.

During the waiting Raff began to suspect there was more tumor activity developing, but we still had no next move and it stirred up so much anxiety. It seemed like an eternity before our quick consultation at the Atlanta CTCA finally paid off and a door opened. Because of that quick consultation, we not only received the needed follow-up from Dr. Durden, but we also received a path to treat new tumor activity. They accepted her, and we were cleared to go. What a relief!

The tumor activity Raff had suspected turned out to be a recurrence on her vulva again; an alarmingly terrible location for all too many reasons, and the tumors were literally growing by the day. Eight weeks.

How can we wait eight more weeks? The horror was palatable. We were praying for an answer; nothing was working. We still had a lot of work to do and a whole new team to meet in Atlanta. It was a tall order as we had loved our team in Tulsa. We had built trust in not only one, but a group of professionals and it was quite a leap to go do it again. Our hearts still hurt for all those we loved in Tulsa who lost their jobs when that location closed.

It was just a week after we got the news that Raff had been accepted by the CTCA in Atlanta and we were on our way. The experience there felt like an extension of our experience in Tulsa. Renewed hope. Road trips were exchanged for plane trips. It had its perks, and plenty of jerks as well. But all in all, it was good.

We had been battling cancer for years. This was her second big tumor surge. The original tumor site treated in Tulsa was healing remarkably, just as Dr. Durden said. Side note: For two years she had the open wound on her hip where that grapefruit-sized tumor had been. It required daily wound care, multiple times per day. It was expelling dead tissue, blood, and all kinds of gunk all the time. She could not submerge herself in water for any of this time. Also, imagine the self conscious feeling when someone in public noticed the odd bulge in her pants as she limped around. It was so painful. But, those were her cards, and she played her hand with enough grace for all of us

We had been using another integrative care model back in Kansas City but we were clearly losing, so we asked the integrative doctor there for a second opinion. He had high hopes for an immunotherapy drug called Keytruda; and recommended that we consider it as opposed to chemotherapy, however the side effects of Keytruda were pretty terrifying, so we found ourselves unsure of which path to take.

We were so conflicted about using Keytruda, and prayed over and over about it. There just seemed to be some unknown roadblock to this treatment. During the time we waited and prayed, we received more information. What we learned was that Raff had a 60% receptivity to

Keytruda, which on the surface sounded somewhat promising, but our integrative doctor reframed that for us. He said the general population who saw results from this drug were just 5-10% receptive to it. So, Raff's 60% was better than just somewhat promising. It was HUGE. Prayer Answered. We chose to move forward and immediately saw results. The first treatment was dramatic. We flew to Atlanta every three weeks; it took only three treatments to beat the tumors back. She was in much better shape which gave her time to heal and us time to regroup. God literally shined the light right where we needed to go.

"For the Lord gives wisdom; from his mouth comes knowledge and understanding." Proverbs 2:6

All the treatment centers had this no-BS-air about them. Everyone there was battling for life. There was just no room for talking about the weather or politics or any of the other small talk that people waste their time with. Many times the waiting rooms were very quiet, undoubtedly out of respect for those there who were in pain and suffering. Raff and I were always very respectful of the people there; we were often the youngest people in most of these rooms.

Thankfully each time we went to Atlanta, a shuttle conveniently met us at the airport. We were shocked by the number of people who went in and out of the CTCA each day; there was almost a theme-park-like feel. Each time we rode the shuttle we were surrounded by others from around the country who were walking this same road. Some were friendly and talkative, and some not so much. Either way it was understandable. Traveling was a hassle when you were healthy. So much more difficult when struggling with cancer.

On one shuttle trip, we met Cedric. Cedric was wearing a headset, a nice quality, no-nonsense headset. An I-talk-on-the-phone-alot type of headset. Not one of those in-the-ear dealios. This one had the pad on the earpiece, and the long mouthpiece to facilitate lengthy conversations. We wondered what he did for a living. We were trying to piece it together and curious to find out more. As we chatted with Cedric, he told us that he was a trucker which explained the headgear, and he also told us what brought him to the CTCA.

He said one day while he was driving he began having pains all over his body. Because of a headache, he couldn't drive so he laid down in the cabin of his truck. He said he laid there for hours just writhing in pain thinking he might die. He was coming to terms that this might be the end. He asked God, if these were in fact his last moments, to send someone to the truck to find his body so that his family would at least know what had happened to him. In a last prayer, he said he would go anywhere the Lord wanted him, and asked the Lord to take away all the pain. Incredible as it sounded, he said at that moment all the pain subsided. All the pain vanished in an instant. Cedric had just made peace with that being the end. Complete surrender and the pain was gone. He pulled himself back behind the wheel and began to drive to a nearby hospital. He told us he was on a four-lane highway leading a long line of vehicles. There were no cars in front of him, and it seemed no one would pass his truck. Not only that, but the oncoming lanes were clear, too. All the cars had pulled to the side and stopped on the shoulder. He told us that he drove eight miles on a completely clear path. Not one car was in his way. He could not believe the strange scenario. He reached the hospital, managed to stop his truck outside the emergency room doors, opened his truck door, and fell onto the pavement. It was then that all the pain returned.

Cedric later learned that the local police contacted the hospital and advised of a swerving trucker on the highway. That they should be ready for some injuries. Cedric said he thought he was driving as fast as he could to get to a hospital, in reality his rig was weaving, barely crawling along at 20 mph. Without a doubt, he knew the Lord had escorted him to the hospital that day. He allowed Cedric's pain to subside just long enough so he could drive those eight miles to get the medical attention he needed.

Cedric's story didn't end there. There was another unexplainable turn of events. One morning at 3:00 A.M. Cedric had a visitor. He told us one of the doctors came to the hospital specifically to talk with him. At 3:00 A.M. The doctor pleaded with Cedric to stay in the hospital a bit longer, not to let the hospital discharge him because he wanted more time to review his case. Cedric agreed and as it turned out, because of that extended stay and additional exams, the doctors discovered Cedric had cancer. It was impossible to know the outcome if he had been discharged and not diagnosed; but what he knew was that whole sequence of unexplainable events; passing out in his truck, temporary pain relief, a clear highway, the early morning visit, the added exams and case review, the diagnosis; it all lined up. It led Cedric to the CTCA where he received what would be a successful cancer treatment.

Now, back to our shuttle ride. Cedric had told us his story, our minds were blown, and our hearts torn open. The bus stopped at the hotel, Cedric stepped off with us, and our conversation continued. We both talked about writing our stories. I told him that I had been writing for years hoping to chronicle our story for my kids, a hope that became a reality when I finished this book. Cedric had been doing the same, but his writing had stalled with all the cancer treatments; he had lost the motivation to write, and just didn't have the gumption to get restarted. I also told him that I also had been toying around with the idea of a podcast for awhile, and had been asking the Lord to light a path forward for me; and here I was face to face with Cedric and his remarkable story that I would love to tell because I fully believed that it would change people's lives. I think I saw his eyes light up. He said our talk had sparked his fire to write again. We all teared up. Divine appointment? I would say so. It was then Raff and I realized we had been dropped off at the wrong hotel. Hilarious. Clearly a Jesus moment.
Many of the Samaritans from that town believed in him because of the woman's testimony, "He told me everything I ever did." John 4:39
The next day we ran into Cedric in the treatment center. He was there for an appointment, his 90-day full body cancer check. He was obviously nervous. We were meeting with our surgeons to hear about Raff's biopsies. The nerves, oh man. As it turned out, we received great news, then we sat with Cedric as he waited for his turn. His stomach was in knots. He said he didn't want the nurse to call his name.

I still shudder when I think of those moments as we have been there so many times. When the nurse finally came out and called his name, time stood still. We wanted to wait and hear his report but we quietly slipped out of the waiting room. We knew he had several appointments and it would be a while.

At the end of a long hallway later that day, we saw him talking to a receptionist. We were excited to see him but cautious because we couldn't discern by the tone of his voice if he had received good news or bad. As we got closer he turned and saw us and his face just lit up! Our faces lit up! He greeted us with the biggest smile. And, with his arms raised high up in the air he exclaimed, "Praise God!" The three of us stood together and had a party right there in the hallway at the cancer center. Those moments! I'm flooded with emotion and my eyes are filled with tears as I think of that moment. God was right there with the three of us. At our victory party. No doubt. Never once had Cedric said anything about the cancer journey being in his control. He pointed right to God. All signs, everything. We danced, we cried, we celebrated. That moment right there! Joy! WOW!

"The Lord your God is with you, the Mighty Warrior who saves. He will take great delight in you; in his love he will no longer rebuke you, but will rejoice over you with singing." Zephaniah 3:17

| 20 |

A Glimmering Beacon

Ever since I can remember we made annual trips to New York around my September birthday. This particular year we were really celebrating. Raff had not been able to get into water since all this started which broke her heart. Her open wounds were far beyond what she could safely put in the ocean water. But, this year was different. On this trip she was able to get in the ocean, and when she did the freedom and joy that burst forth from her was amazing. She was so proud of her body, all it had endured, and how it healed. It was such a big deal. In fact, I don't remember anything else from that trip. It just stands in my mind as a moment on a pedestal.

Thank You, Cancer

There must be something sacred in salt.
It is in our tears and in the sea. - Kahlil Gibran

You are the salt of the earth. - Jesus

Every time we stepped foot on the grounds at the CTCA we encountered God in a very real way. It was as if He stepped into the light to remind us that He was there. We prayed countless times during that time, and at the moment we seemed to be headed in the right direction. We fully attributed it to God's grace. I know many hundreds, dare I say thousands of people prayed for us; people we didn't even know prayed, too. Talk about humbling. I know prayer moved the needle. We felt it.

During our last trip to the Atlanta CTCA, Raff wanted to take me on a date for the best pizza she'd ever had, outside of Italy, of course. Positano was the restaurant and was it ever good. We enjoyed ourselves like we hadn't in such a long time. Between parenting and cancer treatments, finding some moments to relax together was quite the task. It was so nice, and it was on the back of receiving such great news at the center.

As we sat there an older gentleman stopped and struck up a conversation; he asked if we were Italian, would we like some biscotti, and were we from Atlanta? He wasn't intrusive at all. Just very kind and genuinely interested in our story. We told him about our family history, accepted the delicious treat to go with our espresso, and told him why we were there; that we would be leaving in the morning to head back home. He offered his phone number and said to call him next time we were in town. As he left we noticed his tears, and we both teared up. Something happened inside that brief conversation that connected all of us. Looking back, we know God was there.

While we waited for a Lyft to the hotel, I set up my phone to capture that memorable meal, and Raff spotted a dime on the ground. When her family finds a dime they consider it an important sign. It caused her to think of her grandfather who she knew was watching over her. That he was there at that moment.

"But now, this is what the Lord says - he who created you, Jacob, he who formed you, Israel: "Do not fear, for I have redeemed you; I have summoned you by name; you are mine. When you pass through the waters, I will be with you; and when you pass through the rivers, they will not sweep over you. When you walk through the fire, you will not be burned; the flames will not set you ablaze." Isaiah 43:1-2

The next day our flight home was leaving around noon, however, all was not complete. There was one piece of vital information we did not have. A biopsy to put the final stamp of approval on our path forward. But with a noon flight it was looking like we wouldn't be able to get everything done. We hit the ground running in the morning when we got up, urgently asking around hoping to get scheduled for the biopsy. We were willing to delay our flight, get another, or whatever we had to, just to get the biopsy done that day so we didn't have yet another trip back. Thankfully, in the knick of time, just before we had to leave for the airport, we received a call. They were able to get the biopsy scheduled for the following morning. Just one more night's stay. Not another full trip! We thanked the Lord for that last minute arrangement. With the change of plans we had nothing to do for the rest of the day and that evening. So, of course, what else should we do but call the gentleman with the biscotti, our new friend from the previous day.

He and his wife picked us up that afternoon and drove to their ranch just outside of Atlanta. They had built a tremendous Italian villa atop a gorgeous hill overlooking their ranch in a sprawling valley. They were in their 70's and we were both in our 30's; but, despite the age difference we had the best time sharing about our lives, our families, and our faith. We told them our story, and they told us some of theirs. It was so strange, and yet felt as if it was by design.

We stayed at their ranch and visited for a couple hours, then enjoyed dinner at another local Italian hotspot. I particularly remember that we held hands and prayed before dinner. Not awkward hand holding, just very organically woven into the moment. The conversation never ceased. We had a ball. Another wonderful night out. We not only had one great date, but now we had two in a row. Unbelievable!

We said our goodbyes with tear-filled hugs when they took us to the hotel. We felt deeply connected. Strangers 48 hours before now old friends. Amazing! I had no real explanation for the realness of these people and our connection with them. It just materialized right out of thin air. We now have some very good friends in Atlanta who are older than our parents, which makes us smile. Plus, we have a standing dinner date anytime we are in town.

When looking back, these individual moments are all so beautifully connected. A patchwork, if you will, of relationships sewn together with love. Real. Authentic. Experiencing the emotions of each of these encounters, and walking through these moments was breathtaking. We just kept laughing at the enormity of His grace.

"Don't forget to show hospitality to strangers, for some who have done this have entertained angels without knowing it." Hebrews 13:2 [NLT]

| 21 |

Mama, It's Beautiful!

Now, Raff was moving pretty slow and labored on this day at the Atlanta CTCA. She used a walker, and couldn't sit comfortably anywhere due to the location of her tumors. We were on our way to an appointment, made our way into the waiting room, checked in, and found the most appropriate place to sit, if you could call it sitting. This room was full of suffering; there were probably 30 people and half of them looked horrible, the others were their caretakers and some of them looked terrible, too.

As we were waiting, the oddest thing happened. The elevator doors opened and two women stepped out who looked like movie stars. They were dressed in the brightest colors just as you would imagine an African dance team. Their wide smiles looked like they had slept with hangers in their mouths and their magnetism was undeniable. Pure joy. I have no idea where they were from, but all eyes were on them.

It was clear they were on a mission as soon as they stepped off that elevator. Walking past 10 or so people they came directly to Raff. They prayed for her, and told her Jesus was with her. They smiled and hugged her. And then they left. They didn't talk to anyone else, and there were plenty of people who needed some prayers and uplifting. But, as I said, they were clearly there on a mission to connect with Raff. Then, they were gone. We had so many thoughts. Questions. It was impossible to deny that God was orchestrating that moment. When those women appeared, they were so colorful and full of joy everything else in that whole room faded to shades of gray, even seemed to disappear. It was surreal. If it would have just been me, I wouldn't have thought it was real. A dream maybe? Maybe a vision? But Raff was there, too. We both experienced it.

"Are not all angels ministering spirits sent to serve those who will inherit salvation?" Hebrews 1:14 [NIV]

Do not waver in courage due to a statistic.

A statistic is a VERY small picture with very specific parameters in which the results provide some information. A statistic does not represent the uniqueness of your being and in no way could possibly touch the pure MOFO magic that unfolds within you every millisecond of everyday.

If you are currently dealing with a doctor who spews statistics at you without giving you an appropriate lens to receive but not embody that statistic, RUN.

If you are in the care of a doctor who believes in statistics over miracles and the body's ability to heal, RUN.

Miracles happen.

Healing happens.

Mama, It's Beautiful!

Stand firm and grounded in trust.

Raff was getting out of the bath one day, and Ace showed up in the bathroom as kids do. She was the curious type, always just around the corner, and anything wound-related was up her alley, unless it was her wound of course. Ace came right into the bathroom and the following unexpected, unforgettable interaction took place.

"Her hand slowly moved closer to the scar tissue that covers the grave site of the tumor. The area of my body that was so deeply feared by so many, the area of my body that began a death and rebirth of my soul.

Her hand moved closer as the towel covered the rest of my body. Her eyes looked up as she asked "Can I touch it, Mama?"

"If you feel comfortable touching it, sure love. It doesn't hurt."

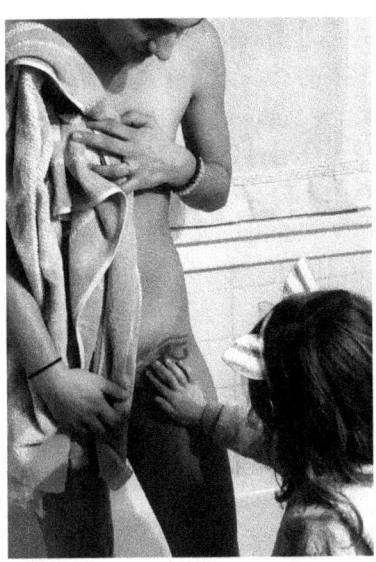

Her hand moved closer, along with her face as she looked at the different skin colors, the "ditch in the road", the crevices of skin that have grown over what once was a severe open wound. A tu-

mor, a tumor with multiple openings, a wound, and now just a "ditch in the road".

An area of my body I could care for but would not dare look in the mirror to view. A wound that left me feeling deformed and gutted by the magnitude of it's morph.

"It's beautiful." She softly said as she touched the surface.

"Mama, It's BEAUTIFUL!"

> There was so much healing and rebirth in this story. God just kept delivering. Our children were His voice.
>
> "Whoever welcomes one of these little children in my name welcomes me; and whoever welcomes me does not welcome me but the one who sent me." Mark 9:37

Raff was the quintessential mother, through and through the mother to all. She cherished that role. Then to have her reproductive system repeatedly ravaged by tumors, deformed by them, cut on by blades, sewn up, radiated, and blasted with chemo. To have this woman, stand there in the shower, and patiently allow her child see and touch the wreckage, and call it beautiful was so healing. I don't think I will ever fully understand. But let me tell you this was one of our most profound moments.

| 22 |

October - Change of Course

In order to pick up a few critical stories I am going to turn back some pages of the calendar to our time at the ranch between treatments in Tulsa and those in Atlanta. My days were full managing the cattle and the property and in exchange we lived in a big house on acreage as part of my pay. Raff was healing from the chemo and radiation. During all this craziness we noticed that we were all just kind of congested, and couldn't get better. In fact, I was having to sleep sitting up, because of the congestion and my asthma. I literally couldn't breathe if I laid down at night. The kids were constantly sick, and Raff of course had her own scenario.

We decided to search for the cause and started with mold testing, for the house and for me. Come to find out we had severe mold problems in the house, and I had severe mold problems as well; when my lungs were tested, although I don't recall the medical specifics, I do remember being told my score was 368, many standard deviations out of the normal mold concentration range of 25-109. The same mold that was choking me was also found in very high concentrations in the house.

We asked that this be remediated immediately. I sent a notice by email to the owners on a Sunday, and on Tuesday, within 48 hours, we got a response that they wouldn't remediate, and that my contract was being terminated. I couldn't wrap my head around what had happened. Raff was in the house with stage four cancer, I was not sleeping because I could hardly breathe, the kids were sick, and we had no money to speak of as the ranch pay was very low; then, we lost the job and the house on the same day. I can't describe the panic in my heart. To have your wife fighting for her life is one thing, but to have the carpet ripped out from under us, was a whole new level of scared.

We had seen miracles, however, in the midst of a crisis it was hard to keep that in mind and stay calm. Days before this all came down, before we had any idea that we would lose my job and the house, we had made an appointment to look at a fifth wheel camper that was for sale. The appointment happened to be on the day after my contract was terminated. Despite the uncertainty and our state of shock, we kept the appointment. It made sense, right? I don't know, but as we looked at the fifth wheel, it began to dawn on us that this might be an answer to a huge problem. Maybe keeping the appointment did make sense. The owner asked if we were interested. Reluctantly, knowing our situation, we said, "Yes. It was amazing." Then she dropped this glitter bomb. She said that she had discussed it with her husband and they just wanted to give it to us, for no charge. They just wanted to help our family. Hard to believe, but this is the truth. We almost passed out right there. We had a place where we could sleep! The celebration began.

We returned to the ranch to begin our move out of the four-bedroom house ditching all the overflow of stuff we had mindlessly accumulated. This was not our first move into an RV; we had experience, but not this fast, nor under this much stress. We took only what could fit and gave away or burned everything else. We had a bonfire, couches, tables, dressers; anything that would burn, we burnt. Literally burnt the ships. We completely cleaned out in 10 days, and moved into the camper. Presidentially downsizing.

And, that was not all of it. The day after receiving the free camper, we were gifted a place to park it. A friend of ours from one of Raff's homeschool groups heard about what had happened. They owned a small acreage with one RV parking spot, and, oh, by the way, it just became available. They gave us that spot to park the RV. We could live there adjacent to their home on five acres for free. Free. And, did I mention that they were friends, both pastors, and they had two kids? They welcomed us, our two dogs, our two kids, and our new free fifth-wheel. This all happened in one day. We moved onto their property and sealed friendships that will stand forever. As if that wasn't enough, this living arrangement also led directly to my next job, and getting us back on our feet. How crazy was all that? Over and over again. We were blessed.

So, winter came. If you've lived in Kansas City you know how cold it can get. We had been living in the camper for months, two adults, two growing rambunctious little girls, and two dogs. The words OVER IT summed up our sentiment. As I was cruising through Craigslist one day, I found an affordable rental house with a big yard and a huge sunroom; it was perfect. We jumped right on it, and within weeks we had the house. Were we ready? Well, I don't know if we were, but we needed the space, we needed a real warm house to live in, and this place just fit. Our next chapter had a home.

Our girls started school. It was a part-time Christian homeschool cooperative situation that was just up our alley. When the school found out about our situation, they offered our girls full scholarships, an amazing and timely gift, and those scholarships continued all the years they attended this blessing of a school. There they developed friendships that have outlasted the years, our relocations, and all of our hurdles.

I don't remember when but we had this growing awareness and curiosity about how and why we received help and answers that seemed to come out of nowhere. I don't think it started from a singular moment; it was more gradual. When we first started noticing and would talk about those incredible moments, we were told to write them down. I wasn't sure why. Maybe to just remember, or maybe to track a pattern for something? I don't know. But we never really wrote down each and every one. I just pulled from our writings and my memory the best I could as I put out our book together. I am quite sure there were many more. But as those moments piled up, many being more incomprehensible than the ones before, we wondered what exactly was going on. We would just look at each other somewhat perplexed knowing that all of them could not be simple coincidences, serendipitous occurrences, or chance. Maybe some, but not all.

"Therefore I tell you, do not worry about your life, what you will eat or drink; or about your body, what you will wear. Is not life more than food, and the body more than clothes? Look at the birds of the air; they do not sow or reap or store away in barns, and yet your heavenly Father feeds them. Are you not much more valuable than they? Can any one of you by worrying add a single hour to your life? And why do you worry about clothes? See how the flowers of the field grow. They do not labor or spin. Yet I tell you that not even Solomon in all his splendor was dressed like one of these. Matthew 6:25-29

| 23 |

We Move Together

To the man who has held me in ways I never knew I needed.

To the man who has listened in ways that has created a home for my feelings, when they can feel so big that I will explode.

To the man who stands in integrity at all times and does not falter, yet still leaves room for growth-craves growth.

You the Sun to my temporary Tornado

This time last year, I was leaving to go to the Cancer Treatment Center in Tulsa, OK unsure of when I would actually come home to be with my family.

I look at this picture and feel sadness in my heart for the pain we all felt. The confusion, deep uncertainty and heartbreak.

What I also see in this picture is a resilient family unit who held space for one another as the uncertainty of cancer tore through us like a tornado tearing literal walls down in my body.

This year, we moved (again) into a home that we can make our own for as long as we wish to make it our home. Danny has found a job, I am not in a treatment center, the girls are thriving. This year, we laugh in bed next to one another and giggle, we cuddle and play, we cry out of joy and out of relief, and as a release.

I don't know where we will be for next year, I dream (a lot). I plan and create but mostly I breathe and play. Some have asked what my "status" is at this point in regards to remission. I am not in remission, but I am healing and happy and my family is together. So we goo000000000d. Cheers to L I V I N from a place of peace while acknowledging that this life is bananas!!!!

I want to savor moments with all my senses.

To smell the tea in the morning as the light comes in through the window, as I listen to the girls giggling. I want to touch the warm mug and take a deep breath in to honor the day. In the moments of pain, of the visceral memories that arise in my body, I want to savor the nausea that arises, I know it will pass, it always passes but even in the savoring of discomfort I can praise the healing in my body, mind, and soul.

Feb 22
Almost two years ago, I began my journey with MISTLETOE therapy for the purpose of aiding healing and treating a cancer diagnosis.

One months after my initial use, I stopped treatment.

After a re-occurrence a couple months ago, I have decided to use Mistletoe Therapy as an immunotherapy for cancer.

MISTLETOE DIARIES is my journey using mistletoe (AKA Iscador, Viscum Album) to aid my body in treating cancer Yes, it is the mistletoe you may kiss under at CHRISTMAS time and it has some incredible properties other than setting the mood for a smooch.

The more I learn about this plant, the more amazed I become at it's power. The more I EXPERIENCE this plant, the more I appreciate it's gentle power.

If you know someone who has been sent home to "get their affairs in order" or if you know someone on a cancer journey— take a look at Mistletoe and it's use as an immunotherapy.

This is my journey, along with some educational tidbits, and an effort at keeping better track of things this time around. I pray that this is helpful to others going on a cancer journey, frustrated with the system, or for anyone who is just interested in the power of plants.

Welcome to the Mistletoe Diaries. I hope you tag along

We decided to take Ginger, our red heeler home after I was diagnosed with cancer. We knew Danny would be away from the girls more, and from Cece our other dog. The dynamic of our family changed quickly but having little Gingy around helped in more ways than I realized at the time.

Yesterday, R became overwhelmed and tired and as she sat down on the grass, Ginger did the same. I don't recommend getting an animal to fix your problems, they don't - they sometimes make it worse. That being said, they can also bring such joy and peace during crazy amounts of adversity.

I love that they have moments like these together. My escape artist and my gentle soul together.

| 24 |

Deer Conversation

We had moved from the fifth wheel and were sitting in the living room of our warm sun porch home having one of those talks like when we were first dating. It just goes on and on. Dreams, laughs, this and that. Reminiscing over the past years, how crazy this journey had been, and Raff sharing so many of her Jesus moments. In my mind, I started to have this poor-me moment. *Jesus, you show yourself to her all the time. What about me? How come you don't show yourself to me?* My thoughts were all in my head. I did not speak of them. Then out of nowhere, through a gap in the curtain beyond the pillars on the front porch, I saw this huge deer walk into our front yard. Now, for perspective, we lived in the city, homes, businesses, suburban streets, highways, all the things. And, I looked and there it stood. I hadn't seen a raccoon, even a squirrel, and this big ol' deer was just standing there. Clear as day. I pointed it out to Raff and confessed to the dialog in my head. She told me, "Look up the meaning of a deer." I scrolled on my phone, and read the words: Jesus himself. I guess I needed something unmistakably obvious, or maybe I really hadn't been looking and listening.

| 25 |

Here We Are

Feeling emotional today as I reflect on the past year.

This time last year, I was crippled by a cancer diagnosis and all the different treatments I had undergone. My body healing but going through a literal MASSIVE loss (and good riddance to the mass!)

This year I am M O V I NG this body and celebrating every single movement. Yesterday, I attempted a snatch for the first time and ooooweeee (form not perfect) but WHAT???

Movement aside, these emotions are still up and down as I my family process, grieves, celebrates, and continues to look for answers both internally and externally.

I don't know everything, I am learning so so much as I go-but one thing I do know is that you don't let anyone dictate your life for you. You have the mofo power to L I V E in every moment.

If you need clarity through chaos, reach out. It is possible.

Mar 22
A cancer diagnosis does not mean you will be bald. In cancer culture, we often see commercials of women wearing pink shirts with their heads covered, or children in commercials with hair loss. It leaves people without life experience, or cancer experience, or education, assuming that every person with a cancer diagnosis will go bald.

The hair loss is due to chemotherapy, but it is not a result of ALL chemotherapy. It depends on type of chemotherapy prescribed, as well as dosage. It also depends on the state of health the person is in when chemotherapy is administered- and many other factors as well.

It is not a given.
A person or child who is bald or is experiencing hair loss, is not always a cancer patient, or a person undergoing chemotherapy. There are other reasons why a person would experience hair loss.

Cancer culture has painted a picture of weakness associated with hair loss, when it may have nothing to do with the actual cancer diagnosis or cancer at all.

May we stay silent and show kindness with no assumptions about one another. Don't ask a woman if she is expecting, don't ask a person experiencing cancer, "how their hair grew back so soon."

If you didn't have the pleasure of knowing Raff, you wouldn't be privy to this little piece of information. Despite harrowing pain and ridiculous amounts of resistance, her beautiful compulsion to help others and care for them always made its way out. It changed throughout the years, but she was always giving of herself, even when I would tell her to stop for her own good. I believe her soul just laughed and was like, "Man, that's why I'm here."

She was a wizard with children. If there was a room of 100 adults and you turned busloads of kids loose in that room and gave them 10 minutes, they would all be hangin' out with Raff. She created a breathwork course for parents and kids called *Breathe-Shake-Shout*. This course was a way for caretakers and children to regulate their nervous systems using their breathing. It was built on biology, attachment, and release, and she nailed it. She used it, she lived it, our girls got to be present with her, and they experienced it. She was so proud, and I am so proud of her for creating it.

I realized that yes, teaching classes and getting simple tools out there is my goal! But DAAANGGGGGG to see it out into practice on the most basic level, literally just speaking and acting on the words "Breathe, Shake, Shout!" In that moment. Wooooo I shed a tear.

We were getting ready to leave the house and it got a little crazy for

Thank You, Cancer

a moment. Then I heard the girls yell, "Breathe, Shake, Shout!"

I looked over with so much joy in my heart. They chose to Breathe, Shake, and Shout out during a transition that could have ended in upset.

Well here we are, again. It's been a little quiet as life has thrown another curveball our way.

Two months ago I had a re-diagnosis of cancer. I have no doubt that I will just fine but it has taken it's toll on me. I used to share more about this whole cancer journey but as time has gone on, I stopped sharing so much- ready to move on with life and having months here and there with glimpses of life without a tumor in my pelvic area. I stopped sharing with all and chose a few, I could stop mid sentence and quit the conversation or pour my feelings out with the select few. It didn't feel SO big, I didn't have to answer so many "How are you feeling?" with people who may not be able to hold the full weight of the answer- or the emotions, or the bluntness. I didn't share mostly because I have been ready to move on from this for a while.

My body has other plans and is taking sometime to catch up.

I have an amazing team. I have an amazing community. For that I am so deeply grateful. To every person who has stepped in, who has stepped up to our doorstep, or a phone call away— thank you.

Danny created a gofundme linked in the bio. The cost of cancer is dreadful and spans much farther than just the immediate medical bills. The cost of supplements, care fo the girls... the whole thing is mind blowing and at times infuriating.

If you feel called to contribute to the gofundme, thank you so so

much from the depths of my heart- for those who have reached out and brought us a home cooked meal, sent packages and who care for our girls, for those who have showered us in prayer and love, ...thank you doesn't begin to touch the gratitude we feel for each one of you who show up for us.

I'm going to go back to posting smiley faces and all the other things that happen in my life.

Raff became less and less mobile as time went on, so getting up and down to help the girls was out of the question. I was still working and not yet a full-time caregiver. But, it was becoming clear that we didn't have the capacity for me to work full time, to care for Raff, and to care for the girls. They were in the homeschool coop, but for only two days a week. We needed help but didn't know where to turn. We were searching for a solution to manage all that we had on our plates, and had racked our brains for any path forward. I'm not sure what took us so long but we finally joined hands and prayed for God's provision. I don't remember exactly when or why it started but holding hands and praying had become a natural expression of our solidarity, the united front in our relationship with each other and with the Lord. Incredibly, the next morning Raff had a group text waiting on her phone. One of our friends had messaged asking if anyone needed help with their kids because she needed a little extra cash and had time to spare. I kid you not. It was as if God said, "There you go. Don't wait so long to ask for help." We again had tears of disbelief and joy. This friend watched our girls for a long time, and she and Raff became even closer friends. We all became closer.

"Ask and it will be given to you; seek and you will find; knock and the door will be opened to you. For everyone who asks receives; the one who seeks finds; and to the one who knocks the door will be opened."
Matthew 7:7-8

| 26 |

Life is So Good. So, So Good

Last night we woke up at 1:30AM for a tornado warning. We ran to the basement and didn't fall asleep until about 3AM.

The night before, pain hit me in the middle of the night and created some challenges in getting back to bed. Wednesday's are our hike days with friends, immersed in nature.

Prior to this whole cancer diagnosis thing, I would have just layed in bed exhausted and probably in a bad mood from the lack of sleep and discomfort.

This morning I woke up, exhausted but SO excited to get in nature with friends. An opportunity to heal WITH my children after months of being knocked off my feet, away at a treatment center and heavy stuff.

Thank You, Cancer

Today we was freaking M A GIC A L!! It was healing to my soul. As @dr.cassiehuckaby often says, your life is your medicine. Today was the perfect example of the medicine of the forest, watching a mother deer come so close to us while eating from the leaves of trees, as her doe watched us curled up close-by.

A turtle walked on the path and the girls watched, waited, and sat silently watching.

The mothers laughed in the stream and held out hands to one another as we helped each other from slipping down hills in mud.

When you live with chronic illness, when you're used to waking up struggling- your mindset matters. It won't be perfect everyday, it doesn't make everything magically disappear but it changes the energy in which you live out your day.

If you're a woman, or mother struggling with your mindset, please reach out. I would love to walk alongside you and encourage you along the way.

As a mother, healing and wanting to do life WITH your kids

- ask yourself. How can I create an opportunity for healing, together? It can be on a blanket reading together, playing cards in the sun, a hike... there are so many options.

Cheering you on
Today I cried at the park, in the car, and at both dance classes out of joy. My kid was crying in the back about wet pants and I was crying because I felt so grateful to be able to experience that little moment with her. Last year, I was on the couch asleep and/or in pain most of the day. Today is so so far from that moment— in every way.

This life is so good, so so good. Don't let anyone or anything tell you different. Breathe.

Cancer is like an onion. If you peel back the layers, on the outside are the symptoms, clinically speaking, a cancer diagnosis.

When you continue to peel back the layers, there is also Cancer of the mind, the heart, the spirit. There is a cancerous energy that wreaks havoc on the physical body, leaving it vulnerable to environment.
Hearing a cancer diagnosis is crippling; fear, sadness, helplessness all come bubbling up to the surface. The immediate recommendations are to attack the cells, in some way.

The last aspect of cancer, if ever acknowledged, is the one that riddles our minds and souls. If we don't address the cancers of our minds and souls, ie negative self talk, shame, deep sadness, the physical healing will be limited and blocked.

In the past few weeks to a year, I have noticed women in their thirties who have received a diagnosis of cancer. I don't know if it is because I am more sensitive to the issue and hyper aware or because it is happening more and more. Young women are being diagnosed with cancer, many of them are mothers.

I know cancer effects humans of all ages, stages, ethnicities, races, anyone is susceptible to varying degrees. There are many different treatments and ways to go about healing and the journey is so specific to each human, each case, the individual and family circumstances. It feels like there are so many variables, so many obstacles to keep into account.

The one thing that is the most powerful and the greatest variable that we can control is our mindset. A cancer diagnosis rocks your world in ways you never imagined, let alone as a young woman.

The really cool thing we can do and have the power to do is accept where we are on our journey.

A big fuck you, crying in bed, holding your chemo or vitamin C bag on the metal stand while you go to the bathroom, hugging your family- every single bit.

Acceptance does not mean you lay down and succumb to cancer, it doesn't mean you passively move along your journey or give up. You accept it and you use the adversity that is in your face and use it as a tool towards empowerment; an opportunity for true, to the core- in your gut metaphorically and literally, DNA changing type of healing.

That vulnerability holding the hand of strength type of healing that reaches everyone around you and proves to neighbors and doctors, family and strangers that healing is absolutely possible.

---

grief from the passing of friends who understood and supported me in my dreams and in my sorrows
grief from loss of friendships that you thought were so deep, where your lives were entangled
grief from the mourning of your self, over and over again as you become renewed.
grief from the loss and change of sexual expression due to the disruption of illness

grateful to have had supportive male figures who understood the struggles of cancer, laughed and cheered m on through and through
grateful for the lessons learned in friendship and even more grateful for the friends who grow with you rather than run from discomfort
grateful for the opportunities to reflect, mourn and renew my soul,

and regenerate this body. the power of it all
grateful for a man who sees my soul rather than just the physical, for the opportunity to grow with my husband in such intimate ways, to learn new ways of self expression.

there is grief. I recognize deep grief... but the gratitude.

The gratitude digs deeper into my soul.
coherently breathing and embroidering through it all ^

27

December

We went to a holiday party. I'm V proud of myself, of us. My body has changed so much these past three years.

Honestly, getting ready for the party and leading up to it, had me all in my feels.
The "I'm so proud of my body" mixed with "What even fits at this point?" but here we are — this is where I am at and once I pulled myself together it felt SO good to gain a greater sense of self.

Thank you @dannylesslie for ALL the patience.

―――

As I opened up about embroidering to peeps, I wasn't expecting so many orders, so quickly. As I've been paying more attention to my breath while fulfilling orders as well as through the day— what I thought would be anxiety turned into SO much excitement!

Through the whole cancer healing journey I have prayed for a way to create, bring joy to others, while also respecting the ups and downs of healing and the very real need to rest. It feels like the perfect fit to encourage others to breathe through challenges but realllilly to sprinkle some embroidered smiley faces and uplifting words, on upcycled denim and other clothing items.

Thank you for all the support!

Reflections
Calcium :
The other day I was reading nutritional facts and read the word CALCIUM. I stopped in my tracks as a flashback slapped me in my face.

It was a pivotal moment in my care and in the seriousness of disease. The IVC that should have given me a boost felt draining. It all felt even more draining. I was told to stop eating calcium. There was too much in my blood. I knew there was a shift as I became light headed easily, confused, no appetitive, constant thirst... hypercalcemia.
Cancer and calcium.

Off to the treatment center.
How ironic to hear so much about the importance of calcium, yet in this moment calcium was an enemy. Hooked up to an IV almost immediately with the purpose of stopping calcium from being pulled from my bones.

Checking my food for levels of calcium. No more salmon, for now.
Drink those fluids. Check those kidneys.
Calcium and cancer, huh. Who knew?

December

Breathe.

What else is on the shopping list?

Reflections :: My husband came across photos of the tumors. When we were in the thick of it, we took photos almost daily to send to doctors, to try and make sense of such rapid growth and the whole situation.

He walked over to me and told me he found them on his phone. We both stood there silently. Thoughts running through my head. He asked if I wanted to see them and I stumbled over my words—- "No! no! Wait, yes. I'm going to puke. No. Yes."

I eventually looked at the pictures and was reminded of the rapid progression of the tumor that was once invisible to the naked eye that grew to be larger than a grapefruit. The damage that it created, the storm in my pelvis and then the break—- and then I looked down. I looked down at the beautiful, deep, multi-pigmented scar tissue that sits on my hip, in my groin. I think to myself, how amazing. How absolutely amazing the human body is. In the moments of fear, I look down and think, "We've got this. I came back from that? Lord, you've got this."

I didn't want to be reminded of the agony and pain that those moments in my life brought not just to myself, but to my family. Our bodies and brains protect us well. I didn't think I was ready. Yet the reminder.... The reminder was so necessary.

BE by @common on replay.

"The present is a gift and I just want to BE."

The girls patient and loving. My mind fighting the panic that

comes with little upsets in my health, at this point.
Sinking into that deep knowing that this bodily feeling will pass just as the emotions do. A reminder and thank you to my body to slow down.... like W A Y down.

Thear you.

I feel you.

———

Can I stay in neutral as my child acts like a child? Can I breathe and let them argue or bicker without getting involved and staying focused on myself?
She will get out of my face.
Their bickering will pass.
The moment will pass.
The laundry doesn't have to get done right now.
Dinner can wait ten minutes.
Everyone is safe.
It can all wait.

———

Do you have a place that is your safe, quiet place? Some people have a closet, a corner or little gardens. In the past few years, the shower has become a place of peace.

A place where I practice coherent breathing and will not be posting any shower shots.
Two things that have brought me peace while healing.

- Breathing in the shower while imagining a waterfall washing away the day and bringing light and perfectly structured water to heal to my cells.

- Embroidering on upcycled denim. I have a LOVE for denim, thrifting and focusing on my breath while embroidering.

I am taking orders but will not be able to begin filling them until December due to previous orders placed.
Song of the Day : Jacob Banks ft. Adeline Gold, Samm Henshaw- Coolin'

At 20 years old, I chose to have an abortion.

When healing cancer, I have had to face that decision many times. As I have worked on healing sexual shame, with abortion being a part of that healing— for anyone who wants to fire judgement and hatred towards the
"opposing" side— I pray that you put yourself in that mother, and father's position.

I pray that you understand the choice to move forward with an abortion or without an abortion is one that has forever consequences on the heart, mind, and soul of the humans involved, the child, the mother and the father.
I pray that you step up and support the family, the woman, child and partner involved as they work through whichever decision they made.

I pray that you step out of the social media squares and actually ACT on these enormous emotions you feel, in a productive and KIND way.

There is shame on the woman for keeping the baby, there is shame on the woman for aborting the baby, there is heartache and mental health issues that may arise on both sides of either decision.
Society is full of judgement and absolute minimal support
— ON BOTH SIDES of the ARGUMENT.

Reach a hand and heart out, show kindness and support to one another.
If you are needing support, please DM or find support that best suits your needs.
If you are triggered by the news, take care of yourself and get off until you are able to respond, rather than react.
If you are triggered by social media. Take care of yourself.
BREATHE, friend. BREATHE.

The stories we tell ourselves about the pains, aches, bodily functions, and upsets in our body can drive a positive effect or a negative effect. When we speak words and complaints about our bodies, it continues that same pattern.
Instead of repeating the same "My head hurts again." OR

"There's something wrong with my (fill in the blank" let's get interesting and creative, and fun and switch it up.
If you can shift your perspective to ALL the amazing things that your body is doing FOR you, WITH you, to PRAISE and HONOR all the functions of every cell of all the systems and pathways—you may start to perceive things differently.
I'm not saying to ignore or pretend like something isn't bothering you. Your body is telling you something. Maybe it's telling you to rest, to stop drinking Coke or to end a relationship but we don't need to obsess and continue to repeat pain and agony over ourselves and ourcells.

There is so much more GOOD and POSITIVE happening in your body than negative. The more you can thank your body for all that good good it does to keep you alive, to survive and thrive, the better the mind, body, and soul can function.

From the moment we are born there are stories that are told to us (that are often not ours at all but we end up embodying them) that tell us we need "fixing".

As we grow up in childhood, that pattern continues and once again they are not your stories but the stories and insecurities, the pain of others that gets poured onto us as our growing brains and bodies absorb it all.
Our teen years are full of more projections more rhetoric that we are broken, the medications pushed down throats, the handheld screens flooding the developing brains of teens and younger children spewing bullshit that they need more, that they are not enough.

Maybe you have experienced sexual abuse, or abuse of any kind. Maybe you were deeply injured. Maybe you have experienced deep pain as we do, as humans.

And so the pattern continues, the self-improvement world, the autoimmune world, big pharma, keeping up with the Jones, keeping up with grades, the fucking keeeeeeping up which continues to tell your brain, body and SOUL that you are not enough, just as you are.

That is some straight up damaging bullshit.
Shed it. Shed the skin of others that has grown all over you hiding the PERFECT, WHOLE human being that you are.
As this past week has unfolded and I have come to so many more realizations about myself, and life. The biggest frustration is the constant rhetoric that you are broken, that we are broken.
I was diagnosed with cancer. I AM NOT BROKEN.

I could continue with past diagnosis and incidents that at one point would have made me felt "broken" but I am not.
Neither are you.

You are not broken. You do not need to be "FIXED" You are GOLD full of light and mofo magic.

MAKE
YOUR
CHOICES.

It has been almost two years down this cancer journey.
When it comes out in conversation that I am thriving with cancer people ask about my "treatments".
These days my "treatments" are simple, gentle, and effective. They are not aggressive like radiation, chemotherapy or more surgery. They are not part of the typical cancer patient's protocol, but they are mine. They have been chosen for MYSELF and have been made with my TEAM.

There is no one size fits all. No therapy, conventional or alternative is for everyone. No diet, supplement, or exercise routine is for everyone.

Whatever you may be facing, may you make the best decision for YOU and your specific situation.
Get quiet, get in nature, and listen to your soul. If it's still too noisy in your head and around you to hear yourself, keep trying to find quiet and to find yourself amidst it all.

I don't always love the saying "Do you, boo!" but...
"DO YOU, BOO!"

Don't feel pressure from others, shame for choosing something out of the ordinary, or at a loss.

You are light. You are pure mofo magic.

The therapies won't work, the pills won't work, there is nothing that will truly and deeply "work" in healing if you do not believe that you are worthy of healing and living fully.

From chronic illness diagnosis to the next, PCOS to Chrons, to Cancer- I was always looking outside of myself for the answer. I would dig deep internally and a little deeper and a little deeper and let me tell you- I have unpacked multiple anvils of gunk to process. It served me well and it has all attributed to my healing. It wasn't until a cancer diagnosis that I sat face to face with myself and asked myself, "Do I feel worthy and ready to be healed?" The answer gutted me and created an incredible opportunity as well.

Our belief systems and mindset dictate far more than the doctors (both conventional and naturopathic) want to admit and tell you.

l urge you to ask yourself the same question. The answer may be surprising, your body may have a visceral reaction, you may get mad, you will definitely get uncomfortable.

But it is SO worth asking.

If you need support and want to dig deeper, together. I would love to support you on this mindset journey.
If you feel you need professional help such as therapy, please do so. There are so many things we can do for ourselves but with certain traumas, you need that help to process the BIG stuff.
Do you feel worthy of healing? Do you feel worthy of living a FULL, beautiful, healing life?

"We're going on a bear hunt.
We're going to catch a big one.
What a beautiful day!
We're not scared..."

We're Going On A Bear Hunt by Michael Rosen and Helen Oxenbury
The book I read on repeat in the classroom. The book I read on repeat to my children. The book I recited to myself through the past two years. The book I still visit and celebrate with my girls.

Don't underestimate the power of books, role play, music, dancing, and the beautiful tools at our fingertips that on the most basic level, hit the deepest part of our brains, hearts, and souls.
What is a favorite childhood book that got you through challenging times?

28

Death and Rebirth

It was in the first months of 2023 that our beloved guardian dog Cece really took a turn for the worst. She was covered in weird lesions that were just beneath the top layer of her skin. They had an odd feel, like peach ring candies. It never bothered her if we touched them. Some were open wounds. We had tried various doctors and treatments but her condition eventually became unbearable. Her breathing was affected because her nose was full of abscesses and her legs were covered in bandages because she licked the open wounds incessantly. We were so worried about her, especially Raff, as she had really developed a deep bond with Cece. Raff, with her wizardry in wound care, would care for Cece so lovingly and it would just break my heart to watch the two of them as she cared for our dog while at the same time dealing with her own bleeding tumors.

We were devastated when we decided to have Cece euthanized. The veterinarian came to our home, and we all sat in the living room around our sweet Cece girl as she crossed. After he gave her the injection, she hung on for so long. She would not let go, I mean held on a long time, many minutes longer than the vet expected. I believe it was because her love was keeping her there with us, with Raff. She was trying to protect Raff for as long as she could. I wonder, if in some strange way, it was possible that Cece took on those wounds, in an effort to take them away from Raff. I actually believe in some way she did. Something about their connection was undeniable. Their hearts and souls were most definitely entangled. It was always clear. Since the beginning.

Shortly after we buried Cece, we traveled to Costa Rica on a mission trip. My employer had offered to take our whole family. Fully paid. You read that right. A fully paid trip to Costa Rica for our family of four. How could we resist? This was a faith-based trip, to build a house for a local family. To gather and labor in Jesus' name. Youth With A Mission [YWAM] was the sponsor and a group out there in the world making serious moves for the kingdom. A sacred pursuit. The YWAM facility oozed with welcoming family-friendly vibes. Off the beaten path, it was nestled under a tropical canopy. It was amazing.

It became very clear there was a bigger purpose for that trip. A higher purpose. On one of those Costa Rican nights Raff asked to be baptized. This. Huge. Unexpected. She had been wrestling with her faith for so long. She had overcome so much, so much doubt, so much resistance. So many barriers along her faith walk which made this decision all the more powerful.

The whole setting that night was powerfully mind blowing. We had enjoyed a home-cooked meal around a large comfortable family-style table before we moved to the pool. It was very dark except for a string of lights draped around the pool. Tony and his wife Rossela led this magical evening. Rossela's mom was with us too. There was something about her mom. Some connection to God maybe? The Earth? Magnificent things? When Raff, Rossela, and her mother entered the pool there was a luminescence reflecting all around them. The water ripples, the lights, the music. We heard the song *Come On* by Brooke Pointdexter pulsing through the air. It was like the song was playing inside the moment. Emitting from the scene. It was powerful. All consuming.

Rossela's mom spoke in Spanish to Raff, in a way that was ancient and powerful. She was speaking Jesus into her. Words that Jesus Himself would say to Raff, commanding grace and love into her, like the powerful words were directly from the heavens and passing through her. This went on for many minutes. Then, Raff was immersed, dipped back into the water. She came up out of that pool filled with complete joy, all smiles, laughs, hugs. It was glorious!

I was baptized as a child and later as an adult, but this moment in this dark pool was absolutely one of the most powerful moments I have ever witnessed. The song Come On by Brooke Pointdexter will forever live in my heart just as the baptism will. It was absolutely magnificent.

The trip, the homebuilding project, the people, Raff's baptism; it all was a wonderful gift!

CMON :: HOME

These past couple of weeks have been life changing.
We said goodbye to our guardian girl leaving on a life changing trip.
Cece before.
Home for a few and back in the air for more IVs and a visit to show the team the mind blowing healing over these past couple of weeks. Tumors shrinkinnnnngggg-LETS GOOOOOOO!!!!

| 29 |

Coincidence? No Chance.

After our time at the CTCA in Atlanta we chose some integrative treatment options in Kansas City. Methylene blue, vitamin C IV's, red light therapy, and others. Unfortunately, the tumor growth began to outpace the treatment. So once again, we had to look elsewhere. During this time we experienced yet another unexplainable set of circumstances. Raff had been searching for a blood test for over a year. She was not able to find anyone that could administer this test locally. And let me tell you, if there was a person who could track something down, it was her. She was an avid researcher, very focused on all things concerning her health.

I had posted yet another GoFundMe. I dreaded it. I was so tired of asking for help. Yet I did. That night, after the GoFundMe posted, I got a text from a doctor who sits next to me in a weekly men's bible study. In his long text he just happened to mention the test that Raff had been looking for. How could he know? The GoFundMe didn't mention the test; I hadn't mentioned the test during bible study either. How could he know?

When Raff saw the text, her jaws dropped. We messaged back, it was arranged that we'd receive the test the next day, and the bloodwork could be forwarded to the testing lab in Greece. And, oh, by the way, they also said the test was $8000 dollars. WHAT?! $8,000. Of course we didn't have it. Like we were at least $7,900 short! I messaged my bible study friend hoping to buy a little time, but also hinting at our lack of funds. In his response, he said they could give us an employee-type discount which would bring the cost down to $6300. Nice of them, but also an amount we did not have. We were totally short. And, we were sweatin' big time as Raff really needed the test, and it could be many weeks before we would get the results.

I assume if you've read most everything to this point you may be expecting another unexplainable solution just before. Time and again it happened. When we were faced with what looked like insurmountable hurdles, when we were right on the brink, miraculously we received a perfect answer. How does all this happen? We weren't totally sure but here we are again and Raff's phone dinged. One of her dearest friends shared that her church decided to donate their monthly tithe to our family. She wasn't sure of the exact total, but she was pretty sure it was $6300. WHAT?! Now, none of the people in this story had any idea about this blood test. No one knew the amounts. The doctor in my bible study, Raff's friend, and the church members. Nobody. Unbelievably we were given access to the test and the funds to pay for it right then and there. Come to find out later, as this book was coming together, the pastor of our friend's church had decided to be wildly generous with their monthly giving and we were the first recipients. They chose to step out in faith as we did, and God so eloquently joined our paths. We had stepped into the unknown with the only move we knew to take. We were terrified so many times. We prayed every day about all of this. As time wore on, and we had more and more moments like this, the evidence that our story was actually His story became shockingly apparent. Miracles? Undeniably. All these connections were miraculous. Here. We. Are.

"Where can I go from you Spirit: Where can I flee from your presence? If I go up to the heavens, you are there; if I make my bed in the depths, you are there. If I rise on the wings of the dawn, if I settle on the far side of the sea, even there your hand will guide me, your right hand will hold me fast." Psalm 139:7-10

| 30 |

Emptiness and The Filling

In case you needed a reminder today.

When the world can feel so big, so bonkers. If someone cuts you off in traffic or you may not feel seen - you matter.
When the sun shines and the flowers bloom- you matter.

If anyone tries to tell you otherwise, tell them they matter.

I came across this audio and it hit me like whoa. How many times on these "healing journeys" do we over analyze, obsess, and tear ourselves apart. As though if we're not breaking ourselves down to figure out "what's wrong" with us— that we aren't being productive in our healing?

When I was first diagnosed I did this, I went down rabbit holes of research, therapists, hypnotherapists, doctors, more therapists-the constant questioning of the self.

These days, being almost three years into this whole thing - I have learned that there is a point where it is beneficial to sit and reflect, not obsess and tear yourself down but reflect, sure. Then there is a point where it's harmful, when you have uncovered so many parts of yourself, stood in the mirror so many times to face all sorts of sides of yourself that it now becomes harmful.

Sometimes healing isn't about being "active". The searching, the doctors, the appointments, the busy-ness of healing.
I am not broken. My body knows exactly what it's doing. I am doing the best I can everyday and that is enough.
Enjoying life, resting as needed, listening to giggles, receiving love and support, sitting in bed watching the wind blow the trees— life is healing.

I don't know who's words these are or who's voice this is but I SO appreciate them.

May you be reminded that you are valuable— PERIOD. You don't have to strive to be valuable.

After we lost our dear Cece, there was a tremendous emptiness in our house. If you have ever owned a Livestock Guardian Dog [LGD] you understand their huge presence. Cece was half Great Pyrenees, half Saint Bernard. They are so gentle and lovers of the family, and they are fierce protectors against outsiders and threats. Cece slept downstairs on the main level and would bark incessantly if someone knocked or there was sound outside the house. From the other side of the door, it sounded like she was 500 pounds. She had a deep echoing bark for a reason. She was an alarm for us, and let whoever or whatever was outside know that she was there and was ready to defend us. When she died, the silence was gripping. We felt so exposed, our house felt so empty.

Emptiness and the Filling

It wasn't long until we decided to get another LGD. We found a farm that bred these magnificent animals about an hour away. We went just to *look* at the puppies, but knew there was no chance we were coming home empty handed, especially with two little girls in the car. We got to the farm and the friendliest couple came right out to greet us. Everything about them was warm and welcoming including the farm and their LGDs. A picturesque green sheep pasture on the northern slope was where the pups' parents served as working dogs, and adjacent to the pasture was a pen with the pups, 11 or 12 little white puffballs wiggling around everywhere. We knew it was important to observe which pup chose us, and sure enough, one came right to Raff and the girls. This was our girl. I believe there is much to be said about the moment a pup chooses its owner. We found our little girl, rather she found us. We named her Lou Lou, and we took her home that afternoon.

Lou Lou was every bit of a force as our Cece had been and then some. We had Ginger the energetic cattle dog as well, but it wasn't long before Lou Lou outgrew her, began to take the reins, and became the dominant one. So much so that we eventually had to find our sweet Ginger a new home. Ginger's energy and aggressive nature became more than we could handle safely with two little girls and Raff in cancer treatment. You can nurture a dog into being a tremendous pet, but as hard as you try their instinct will just not leave them. Ultimately, we rehomed her to ranch working cattle, her life calling. A sad day, but a needed move.

| 31 |

Lou Lou

Didn't take long for us to fall in love with this puppy after meeting her at a farm.

We were going to hold off on bringing a puppy home but I mean... how do you say no to this mini polar bear.

These past days after another infusion have been hard but having Lou Lou to snuggle and love on has been such a blessing.

I was so against having indoor dogs. When we were on the farm I LOVED having Cece be outside and guard the house.

Moving back to the city she still was our guard dog and would watch over the girls. In the evenings she would sleep by the front door.

The girls give me grief that | "don't love" Ginger, our other dog but

I realize I never had the time to bond with her. She was the puppy we got before I entered the Treatment Center for nine weeks.

This time— this time I get to snuggle this cloud of fluff and spend time with her. I won't be able to wrap her up and snuggle her in my arms for too much longer but I'll spam your insta feed with puppy pictures. Yes, yes I will be that person just for a short while.

| 32 |

Lifelines

This past year has been rich with blessings. It has also reaffirmed the importance of connection to those important in our lives. Our friends and family were the lifelines that we desperately needed just to stay afloat in our day to day. It was all too easy for me to attempt to take on all the burden which was a mistake, and there was no need. Yes, it seemed honorable to put myself alone in the ring, but I had this whole other support system in my life. I had others, family, and God. My ability to be vulnerable with my struggle and our battles were like acorns that could grow into mighty oaks of strong relationships. But only if I was humble enough to use the watering can I had in my own garage to water those relationships through the tough times.

I realized how I had neglected my relationships when I saw a group of guys who I hadn't seen in years, some I hadn't seen in almost 20 years. It wasn't that we didn't care about each other, it was just that life had ushered in so many other things. We all were married, we all had kiddos, and we all had our own issues. But also, we could have each other and that could save us, if we so choose. The renewed sense of spirit that came from that get-together was huge, at least for me. It reinforced the importance of connection. It's safe to say, I needed that time. I realized how important it was to stay connected to the men in my circle.

Throughout this cancer journey, many friends reached out and were a lifeline. I needed reminders of who I was and who I had. All of us should collectively make an effort to be there for each other. As I weathered the storm the difference a phone call made, it could change my head space from night to day. Before a phone call it seemed I could be in a downward spiral, then afterward I could see the sunshine. There was no crazy voodoo that took place. It was simply that I spoke with another guy about what was going on. That simple interaction created such a relief. Not only that, but it happened many, many times and gave me some gumption for parenting, some gumption for work, and even a little left to put some time in for me. The strength that comes from connection is palatable. I can't thank them enough. At the root of this whole game is simply the power of connection. It was literally a drip campaign. The importance of consistency in our relationships, is directly congruent to the forest of our support in our lives.

In the most basic sense, keep up with your friends, if nothing else at least a call every few months. As men we hold important positions in our relationships, but we also need support. This is not a dig on our ability, it's a testament to the magnitude of the journey. We strengthen each other. Let's not walk alone.

A couple other keys which helped me thrive in the midst of the storm were prayer, if that is the route you choose, and intentionally setting aside time for my relationships with my wife and my children.

| 33 |

Unlayering

September came and it was time for our annual trip to New York, to Rockaway Beach to visit Raff's family. Her grandmother was her hero, and this was her town. It was an idyllic town right on the beach, kids riding bikes, running around as the kids in the movie *Goonies*. There was a Mr. Softee's ice cream truck that dropped by every day; all the kids and plenty of adults like us would run out to meet him. The ocean was right there, the skyline of Manhattan was across the bay. It was incredible. A town of firefighters and policemen. A town of families who had been there for generations. They weathered 9/11, they were flattened by hurricane Sandy, yet they carried on. I got to be a part of this place, and it will always live in my heart. It was very hard on the family and especially Raff when her grandmother passed in 2019. A little piece of Raff was lost. From that day, a photo of Raff hugging her grandmother has lived in our kitchen next to her handwritten words "Be Known for The Way You Love." This statement lives in our home, and was cherished in Raff's heart, and now in mine.

I was still working at the job I found through our pastor friend; the friend who many months earlier gave us the free RV space. I was at work the Friday before our trip to New York and a guy from the HR department walked in with a manila folder. The look on his face meant only one thing. They fired me. It was my last day. I could elaborate but suffice it to say I knew that this door needed to close. This termination was actually what I needed to change course. Oddly enough I looked at it as a gift of sorts, an unlayering; a layer of my life, my job layer had been peeled away. I was holding on to that job knowing down deep it was wrong for me. I knew there would be another path. We had seen it over and over and hallelujah for that.

"Consider it pure joy, my brothers and sisters, whenever you face trials of many kinds, because you know that the testing of your faith produces perseverance. Let perseverance finish its work so that you may be mature and complete, not lacking anything." James 1:2-4

In my situation, I believe God gave me a path that I couldn't see. He took away my job because 100% of me was needed in my home for my family. I had a maximum bandwidth each day. In my mind, I had 100% to give each day so I made choices where my energy went and those choices subtracted from the remaining bandwidth available for everything else. If my work took 60%, then I had 40% for the rest of my day. If I somehow tried to use extra bandwidth by borrowing from tomorrow, it reduced my 100% the following day. We were running on deficits anyway because there were so many sleepless nights. When I shifted from full time work to full time caregiver, it was a real eye opener, a huge transition; caregiving was more demanding than I ever imagined. As Raff's health began to fail and she became bedridden, I had to take over the responsibility for the girls, their homeschooling, and all the other domestic tasks in addition to Raff's care. There's no way I could have held down a job, even a remote one, with the demands at home, nor could I have hired help to cover all the bases. But, the change was also a relief because I was able to meet so many of our needs. For the next 15 months after my official break with employment, I was incredibly busy all the time. Fast forward to today and I am so grateful that my path turned.

| 34 |

September - Disorienting Grace

It's been an intense couple of weeks but there has been so much forward motion that has been incredibly encouraging.

Today, I will be trying a new therapy. I am excited, feel so grateful, and also nervous. I never know how my body will react to any therapies— I'm a sensitive strong one they say . Whether it's "natural" or conventional the body is so unique. It processes and assimilates in all sorts of amazing ways.

Some have asked about the "Strong as a Mother" apparel so we started another campaign. If you have a shirt, or sweatshirt - take a pic and tag me or @dannylesslie

It's super encouraging and feels like a big hug knowing yous guys are with me in that distant but close kind of way.
Prayers for ease today are so VERY VERY welcome.

Some days I feel super overwhelmed, like yesterday when my brain was fried and I put my book in the sink with water and a sweater in the fridge. (It's like that, folks)

In the flurry of Raff's care, money was just in and out the door like wildfire. It was very hard to keep track of. For many weeks we had $15,000 each week fly out the door for care alone, not including living expenses. We had doctors' visits, travel, wound care for years, supplements, and scans; it was mind blowing. There was one month where we didn't even have our rent. To be honest, I was afraid Raff was dying, so rent was way down on my list of priorities. It may sound strange, but our lives were in such triage mode for so many years, I began to feel very detached from normal reality. I hadn't even had time to worry about not having rent, nor had I processed the fact that we didn't have it. We were loading up in the car one evening after visiting some friends, one of Raff's best friends ran out after us and said she almost forgot that she had something to give us, and handed an envelope to Raff. It was our rent in cash. It was due the next day. She said they had been saving it up for us. This was totally unexpected, out of the blue. It became harder and harder to attribute any of this to coincidence, to deny the evidence in this story, that it is His story. Scripture says that God feeds the birds. Why would He also not take care of us?

"Then Jesus said to his disciples: "Therefore I tell you, do not worry about your life, what you will eat; or about your body, what you will wear. For life is more than food, and the body more than clothes. Consider the ravens: They do not sow or reap, they have no storeroom or barn; yet God feeds them. And how much more valuable are you than the birds! Who of you by worrying can add a single hour to your life? Since you cannot do this very little thing, why do you worry about the rest?" Consider how the wild flowers grow. They do not labor and spin. Yet I tell you, not even Solomon in all his splendor was dressed like one of these." Luke 12:22-27

I don't think we respect REST. I don't think we know rest or how to rest. We fight it so hard- making it a chore that we procrastinate.

September - Disorienting Grace

In this season, I crave relentless rest. Unceasingly intense rest.

I want to recover my strength intensely by putting a stop to motion and sit in a silence that calms your mind and opens your soul. A rest that deeply regenerates and rewire every cell. I want to know rest intimately so l can never ignore it's quiet but necessary presence in my life again. It's tug on my soul so clear, time to let it be.

Friends would come to visit all the time since Raff was basically not able to leave the house for years. There was another time when we were low on funds and had hardly any cushion, one of Raff's close friends came over to visit, and left a heavy envelope full of cash. More provision.

"All the believers were one in heart and mind. No one claimed that any of their possessions was their own, but they shared everything they had. With great power the apostles continued to testify to the resurrection of the Lord Jesus. And God's grace was so powerfully at work in them all that there were no needy persons among them. For from time to time those who owned land or houses sold them, brought the money from the sales and put it at the apostles' feet, and it was distributed to anyone who had need." Acts 4:32-35

I remember when I first came to terms with using a cane. It was over three years ago and I was barely able to walk standing upright.

I searched hours online for the cane I would actually feel comfortable using. Not too much like a grandma, not too bright, not metal, not this, not that. Any excuse not to actually use one.

I felt that if I gave into using a cane than it would be a downward spiral. It would be some admittance to the severity of my situation. As though I had to admit anything - that walking bent over at almost a 90 degree angle wasn't silent admittance.

I eventually surrendered to canes and wheelchairs as temporary assistance. A little tinge in my heart, the passing thought of "dang, my situation is this..." as I reached for the wheelchair or the cane. In my head I had all sorts of reasons why I couldn't or shouldn't use these tools.

"What will the girls think?"

"They'll think something is really wrong." The thoughts that a mother has while raising children and who's health drastically changes day by day. The girls didn't really care though. They used the canes as props in play and that was that.

A few months ago I picked up a cane again and at first I heard, "Mama has to use a cane again?!?!" "Why is Mama using a cane again?!" — the conversations began. This time I could set my ego aside, accept my reality and be grateful that we had the tools that would allow me to be on my feet longer with the girls. Most days it stays in the car in case I need it and when I do I'm grateful.

I don't want to miss out on my time with the girls. I want adventures and fun and experiences regardless of my health status or "evidence of disease". I don't think the girls associate my health with the cane, or wheelchairs, or those spiffy carts I get to ride in stores if need be.

So much of this journey is mindset. I may not be able to choose every little thing that is happening right now. But I get to choose how I look at life and how I look at things.

These canes and wheelchairs are just tools, period. Not attached to my ability to heal, or motherhood, or my anything. They are tools, and for that I am grateful.

September - Disorienting Grace

I was constantly looking for ways to somehow afford the insane bonfire of cash that our lives had been for the past three years. We always felt like we were running at a pace we could not hold for much longer.

A dear friend and legend in the sourdough trade had family with connections to Chicken N Pickle, a local restaurant with pickleball courts and leagues that booked fundraising events. I reached out to them right away and they generously donated their space for a fundraising pickleball tournament and silent auction to raise money for Raff's treatment. Before the event I spent two months searching for auction donations. It was a constant flurry of emails and phone calls as I reached out to anyone and everyone I could think of.

That day was magic. Financially it helped, as every bit did; but it was also the people, the showing of support. Raff saw just how many people loved her and supported her in this struggle. It was just breathtaking. Friends donated their time, there were balloon animals, popcorn, cotton candy, sourdough, music, games, laughs, and tears. It was magnificent. Watching Raff take all of this in made me so happy. I wanted her to feel loved, and I wanted her to know how much we all loved her, and I believe it happened. I get choked up when I think

Thank You, Cancer

about it, and will be forever grateful to all who were a part of that big day.

In awe and in bed after yesterdays incredible fundraiser @chickennpicklesop
There are not enough words that would do yesterday's experience any justice.
These three plus years have been the hardest of our lives but the most blessed.

Thank you to every single person who showed up, who sent messages of support, who organized. Thank you to @dannylesslie who I think should switch careers and partner with some of the best who showed up.
Thank you
can do it anymore.
for holding us up when we don't think we can.

I know I'm missing plenty others but truly, if you were there you matter more than you know. Thank you

| 35 |

Silence

The news of a good friend passing due to cancer, or complications of cancer- while being a cancer patient yourself hits your core in a way that is complicated and indescribable at times.

It brings up thoughts of death. Deep grief and sadness.

Confusion but also trust. A child, and a grandmother all in the same month. Me—- in the middle of ages, with a rare situation as well. What do you do when the death of a close friend mirrors your situation in a way that few others do.
The mass grows fast. But they're so positive. But there are complications that no one talks about. Why a child? Why such bright lights in this world? So bright. Anger towards God, and then more grief. And silence.

Thank You, Cancer

Silence to hear.
Silence to grieve.
Silence to remember.
Silence to honor.
Silence to surrender.
Silence and determination.

| 36 |

Energy and Trauma

We had been fortunate to cross paths with some unbelievable humans in our day, and this story came about because of some of them, some very close friends, soul-connected friends. Our connection was DEEP and immediate. I spent years in the fitness industry and met Eka there. I spent a long time training him and we became the best of friends; it felt as if we were brothers. Our families met and all of us just felt at home with each other, and it showed. As life progressed and we moved from LA to Kansas, we still remained in contact here and there, but the connection never lost any depth.

Their magnificent son developed a very rare condition that caused a brain tumor. This torrential moment in their lives ran parallel to the cancer journey we were on; it was almost like a bridge between our families that strengthened our bond and connection. Their son and Raff had a crazy connection. He was one of a kind just as Raff was one of a kind. They searched high and low for a cure; but that was his path and tragically they lost him. I cannot express the wave of sadness that moved around the world when he passed on. We had also moved mountains to find a cure for Raff, but that was not her path either.

Along the way, we got a call from our friend Eka. He told us that we needed to talk with a man, whose work was life changing in the best way. He was an Energetic Trauma Healer. We had absolutely no idea what we were stepping into, but we had full faith and trust in our friends, so we immediately scheduled a call with this healer. He was wildly busy so the call was set a month or two out, and we really didn't think much more about it until the time was close.

The healer lived on the other side of the planet, so since our times didn't jive well, the Zoom call was on a Tuesday night around 11 o'clock. Now at this point our kids were five-ish, so 11 was a stretch for us; we could fall dead asleep at dark because of general exhaustion, but we held out for the call. We were excitedly nervous as the time approached, and considering what transpired it was well warranted.

We jumped on the call to a somewhat awkward but very kind man. There was nothing unusual about the way he looked or the way he was dressed, he just had an interesting unusual way about him. It was clear that he was manipulating things in his mind and in the space around him. We just chalked it up to an unfamiliar new experience. There was no questionnaire to complete or introductory questions to provide any background about us either, no fact finding expedition by him to learn about us at all. He did not know Raff's history, nor mine, nor our faith. We were just meeting halfway across the world.

Now I will tell you, before our call, Raff and I had discussed and prayed that God would direct the efforts of this man. Jesus was our only filter in this conversation, because we had no bearing on what was going to happen. Over the past years the evidence that God was leading us through the darkness was increasingly more apparent, so this was it.

We were leary, but also fully in. For the next 45 or so minutes with whatever methods he was using, he told us Raff's story. He told us of all the traumas that had happened to her, when they happened, who they happened with, and so much more. All of these things, he could not have known, in fact I didn't even know all of them. We were astounded.

He told us about her trauma. He said that traumatic experiences will leave imprints behind. Imprints made by the person who caused the trauma. And, those imprints stay with the victim and affect the nervous system in an undeniable way. What he described next was very eerie. He told Raff that she had imprints, or energetic beings, attached to her and had them for years, since childhood. Those energetic beings were like parasites, or leeches or something, but on a soul level. We thought this was a tad far-fetched, but he was literally spot on about all the traumas and her life experiences. He was undeniably correct. I attest that he was right. Then, he presented all of these documents talking about life force, megahertz when she was born, and on and on. It was mind-blowing. We didn't understand it all but we had so many unusual encounters throughout our journey, things like this fit into our brains a little easier.

It was what happened next that was most unsettling. He casually mentioned that he was going to take away all of the spirit beings that were leaching off of Raff's soul. Excuse me, what was that? He repeated that he was going to make them go away. Raff would feel nothing, and neither would I, but he would feel it and the energy would pass through him. Now, wait! You're telling us, you're going to perform some kind of exorcism right now? We were so far out of our comfort zone then. We were shook, like scared shook. I can still feel the vibrations in my chest thinking about that moment. But he calmly confirmed that was what he was going to do.

We were at least an hour into this mind-blowing meeting; it's midnight on a Tuesday and our kids are asleep in the other room. Then he said words that caused tears to literally explode from our eyes. He said, "The only way any of this is possible is if I flood you with the love of

Jesus Christ." Our only filter. Our only navigational beacon. Our only qualifier. It was at that moment we knew that God's hand was in this story, too. The relief we felt was like a warm waterfall all around. I'll never forget it.

He continued and asked if there were any other people or animals in the house, because when those spirit beings are released they will jump into another host, maybe your child or someone else near you. At that, we had all kinds of thoughts and worries charging through our minds. We told him about the kids and the dogs in the other room, but he assured us he would protect them in an energetic way. That was all I knew. Yes, I am aware this is outside the bounds of most normal Zoom conversations, but we were in it, so we intended on seeing it through.

Raff and I closed our eyes and just began to pray as he began. We are laying in bed on our bellies looking at the iPad crying and praying Jesus blood and the protection of the Holy Spirit over us, our girls, our dogs and our home. The healer was calling the beings forth, and when this was happening, the sounds and screams that were coming from him were so disturbing. We just clenched our eyes tighter, prayed harder, and literally were shaking in fear. A few minutes in, hearing the burps, the yawns, the sounds, and the screams, I had to look. I had to see what was happening. I opened my eyes for a moment to see this man contorted to the side, writhing, and making the most twisted and alarming sounds. I immediately shut my eyes. This went on for 10 or 15 minutes, and then finally it was done. This was easily the most intense 20 min of our lives. After that period of, what he called a releasing of the other ones, we returned to conversation.

The calm in the room was piercing. But we were still rattled. He said that the next day Raff would feel very light, and that over the course of 21 days or so she would begin feeling like herself again. There would be a period for about a week that she would feel empty like a huge sense of loss, like something very important to her was missing, and during this time, she had to be careful not to let herself slip into negative thoughts or negative situations, because now she had this empty space that should be filled with life-giving things not things that take away.

Before I continue, it's important to know that Raff's posture had been significantly impacted by the disease. When she was on her feet she had to bend over almost at a 90-degree angle and lean on a walker or cane because her tumors caused so much pressure. She could not sit either as her whole butt and groin were covered in open tumors. The next morning after the call with the healer, I went downstairs to make coffee, and there was Raff standing completely upright. She was sweeping the kitchen floor. "What the heck are you doing?" I laughingly asked.

She said, "I feel great, I feel so light, I don't know, I just felt like cleaning." She hadn't cleaned, let alone been down in the kitchen in months. Something had happened. And, the next 21 days or so fell right into his timeline. Unbelievable, yet totally believable.

The craziest thing to me about this whole story is how this man, who has this wild skill set pulled out the sledgehammer when he said, "The only way this works is if I flood you with the love of Jesus Christ." He hadn't spoken of his faith and never asked about ours. In fact, his approach seemed completely utilitarian, detached from faith. What I experienced was that God is MUCH more than I can ever know. Jesus, the Holy Spirit covers bounds that I cannot fathom. In fact, when I use the word bounds, that's probably a human weak-minded way of trying to put something divine in human terms. The experience clarified for me how boundless He is. It clarified for me the magnitude of the misunderstanding of my understanding. I was concerned that the energy healing would conflict with what we believed; but, little did I know, Jesus was front and center.

I still think of this bizarre experience that is so far from any I've ever had or imagined. I know what I saw and heard, but I guess I'm still not sure what to make of it. I'm also keenly aware that so many of the experiences throughout these past five years did not make sense, seemed impossible, and just beyond any logic. So, for now, I've chosen to just sit with it. All of this exists under Him. This was how God used our struggle to blow the bowlines off our finite understanding of Him. He is so much more.

37

Joy and Love

Some months ago I came across Terry Tempest Williams' work. Her words continue to touch parts of me that feel lonely at times. Though these words are an expression of her own feelings and healing journey of cancer, they continue to speak to me.

I feel like they're pretty relevant to life, for many. Whether it is cancer, chronic illness, or just the challenges of life.

May we listen to the song birds as a reminder that this life is to be celebrated.
"I want to feel both the beauty and the pain of the age we are living in. I want to survive my life without becoming numb. I want to speak and comprehend words of sounding without having these words become the landscape where I dwell. I want to possess a light touch that can elevate darkness to the realm of stars.

Thank You, Cancer

This vascular malformation could bleed and burst. Or I can simply go on living, appreciating my condition as a vulnerable human being in a vulnerable world, guided by the songs of birds. What is time, sacred time, but the acceleration of consciousness? There are so many ways to change the sentences we have been given.

...once upon a time, when women were birds, there was the simple understanding that to sing at dawn and to sing at dusk was to heal the world through joy. The birds still remember what we have forgotten, that the world is meant to be celebrated. "

- Terry Tempest Williams "When Women Were Birds"

It's cancer they said.
That won't work, they said.
You need to move fast, they said.
You'll be on hospice, they said.
No more options, they said.
They said so much, everything except what He said.
what does He say??

On this cancer journey, looking back at before I was diagnosed I realize that I never really allowed myself to be loved fully. I know that sounds cliché or whatever with this whole "love" age that seems so surface until you're so in the depths of a painful situation that you realize, shit— it's me.

I'm learning. I'm still learning how to allow my husband to love me. God, that sounds insane doesn't it. I am still learning how to allow my husband to love me, to let all my walls down, how not to push him away when he just wants to be there.

Last night, my pain meds lapsed while I was asleep and I woke up with shooting pains. He woke up while I was in the shower trying to find relief at 2AM. He checked on me but I figured he would go downstairs and deal with our Pyrenees puppy Lou Lou as he usually does to stop her whining.

He didn't.

I got in bed waiting for the meds to kick in, breathing through the pain and throbbing. I was so focused on breathing that I assumed he already went downstairs.

He didn't.

I told him he could go that I would be ok and that I was just waiting for the meds to kick in.

He didn't.

He laid next to me legs hanging off the bed and said, "I'll wait for them to kick in too"

As I fell asleep I remembered thinking "let him love you".

| 38 |

Grace, and Grace, and Grace

Dr. Jess was Raff's chiropractor and truly an angel. She treated Raff for no charge for years. Every time Raff came back from an appointment with Dr. Jess, she looked like a different person. But, Dr. Jess was more than just Raff's source for chiropractic care, she was a soul connection for Raff. She had her own experience with cancer and was also on an epic journey of motherhood. God was woven stitch by stitch into her story, and He joined those two babes to make for a monumental testament to His love, and a monumental example of His love as well.

Toward the end of our days in Kansas City I remember that we barely were able to make it to Dr. Jess for treatment. Raff was unable to sit and barely able to ride in the car on her back. It almost didn't happen. But, somehow we managed. It goes without saying that money was tight then; we were for sure in the hole since every penny was funneled to Raff's care. After she saw Dr. Jess that day, Raff came out of the appointment in tears holding an envelope that was chalk full of cash. Cash from Dr. Jess. It was already spent, but nevertheless, it was cash that sustained us. The amount is immaterial. Whatever it was it covered the moment we were in.

The eyes of all look to you in hope; you give them their food as they need it. Psalm 145:15 (NLT)

We obsessively searched for answers to what was going on with Raff's cancer. We had kept photo records of the tumor's progress, and it was clearly progressing, but we had no idea what was happening internally. PET scans were usually the go-to. They involved radiation and provided information about metabolic activity; and lit up areas where there was some activity. The activity could be general inflammation or it could be cancer. In the event there was healing going on, which Raff always had to some degree, those areas lit up too and the doctor could identify places with a high likelihood of being cancerous. The problem was, maybe it was, but maybe it wasn't. The only way to really know was to remove a piece of the tissue and test it, a biopsy. Raff did not want to be cut on. Understandably. Therefore, she opted for something different, a Prenuvo scan. The Prenuvo scan could help us figure out what was going on without radiation or a biopsy. The closest place that offered it was in Dallas, TX.

I want it crystal clear that our opinions and our choices should not be construed as medical advice. I am not a doctor and neither was Raff. I'm sharing our decision-making process as it pertains to our specific situation. Each situation is very different. Definitely do your own research. Please.

As always, there were problems we had to overcome. To get the Prenuvo scan, we had to travel to Dallas, a 10-hour drive from Kansas City. Our solution to the distance was a rental van; I removed the seats, laid a futon mattress in the back, and Raff laid on her belly, and slept the whole way. She called it her magic carpet.

The second problem was the cost. $1000. Of course, we didn't have it. We actually had $1000 in our bank account for a brief moment, but we needed that for rent. After much deliberation and prayer one evening, even though we did not have the money to pay for it, we decided to book the scan anyway. I was so worried, literally sweating, but I just felt that this was the move that we needed to make. Unbelievably again, my phone dinged about an hour later. It was a GoFundme email daily update. Email updates normally hit a day after a contribution was made, but, this GoFundMe was drained and had been dead for months, maybe for more than a year. But, here was the update. Someone the day before had placed $1000 in our account. Truth. I am not making this up! I wouldn't! How could this happen? It may as well have been Jesus Himself. There was no question, why or how it happened. I agree that it is totally unbelievable and unexplainable without a supernatural presence. Here We Are trying to make this decision, beating ourselves up, and God already covered it through an amazing human out there. It was another opportunity to trust in God's ability to provide.

"The poor and needy search for water, but there is none; their tongues are parched with thirst. But I the LORD will answer them; I, the God of Israel, will not forsake them. I will make rivers flow on barren heights, and springs within the valleys. I will turn the desert into pools of water, and the parched ground into springs." Isaiah 41:17-18 [NIV]

Took a long drive to Dallas to get a Prenuvo scan. I was dreading the drive but the amazing @dannylesslie made me a bed. So I was basically on a magic carpet ride the whole time and he was my Aladdin.

My Jasmine ass slept like a princess.

We stayed at an Airbnb that had way too many beds in the living room... like a king and two queens, plus two queen bunk beds in another room. I was thoroughly impressed at the use of space.

For those curious about the Prenuvo scan— the space was beau-

tiful and staff was wonderful. We got our own little room where Danny hung out while I got the scan. scan was super loud but they give you an option to Netflix and chill in the space tube or listen to music. It was so loud I just laid down and tried to sleep as the machine made it's hammering noise. It was 30min (others are 60min depending on the scan), I was back in our cute room where I changed and boom, outta there! Snacks provided. Drinks provided. No radiation + sugar provided, win!

A special visit from @lunadobles if to end the trip and I was back with Aladdin on my magic carpet ride home!

We've got a trip to Arizona coming up for a consult. I know I haven't been on here, or my phone much answering peeps. I'll make an update video soon.

Things change fast and it's tiring but there's always joy in the morning.

It was a crisp fall day, but the sun bathed the city with warmth, and we were out for a family date at a coffee shop. Our ritual, if we had one. We loved the time together, ever since we met. We always cherished our coffee shop dates. They were home for us. There was intention there. We were all focused on being together and for us that was the highest priority above all else.

We visited the older part of town that had been revived with coffee shops, restaurants, and businesses. It was just always hopping. We grabbed our festive bevos [beverages] and headed to a nearby park that the girls loved so much. Nestled under huge trees and some towering apartment buildings was this awesome park with amazing structures for the kids, nets, hills, tubes, and slides. Raff and I just kind of meandered, laid on some grass, and watched our girls laugh and rumpus around.

It wasn't long before a girl walked up to us. "Raffi?" she asked. It threw us. Neither of us had ever seen this girl before, Raff hadn't spent much time in KC and we rarely came to this park, so it was odd that this girl recognized her. The girl continued, "I saw your GoFundMe online, and when I saw you I just had to come say hello. Here is all the money I have with me. Please take it. I was so touched by your story, and I want to help you all." We were just frozen in disbelief. Not only were we walking down a path in life where it seems that money was just on fire, God sent this woman to tell us He's got us! Raff and I looked at each other and cried. What a day!I

Give us today our daily bread. Matthew 6:11

| 39 |

The Mirror

It's taken me a while this time around of reoccurrence to share more openly about my situation. I realized once I became so emotional, like S00000 emotional I could barely talk to anyone— that there was a sadness and grieving in my soul that maybe I never allowed to fully arise.

What I feel now, after some reflection and still tears rolling down my face— is that this time around I have hope (it has rarely left), I have a deep belief and expectation of healing, but the doctors we have interviewed don't feel the same.

We still hear "this is so rare" "we don't have data on a case like this" "we can try and treat it like cervical cancer" —-and plenty of other things.

We have our dear Dr. and friends at a clinic here where I have been supported as much as possible within the boundaries of Kansas Law.

On this past trip to a Cancer Center in AZ. The doctor saw me— she called out the GRIT in me and the importance of keeping it through these next months.

I felt seen again— which brought me to tears. The grit that I have maintained— and will continue to do so. She saw my relentlessness, my love for life and people, she saw our marriage and the vitality in it even through all of this. She saw MY data not other's data and created a plan around me, chemo built around me, radiation specific to the tumors, IVs specific to me. She saw the big picture and she saw me.
When I look in the mirror I don't see myself. The weight I have lost. Clothes help me feel a sense of identity. A little make-up helps perk my face cheeks up. My relationship with my husband allows me to curl in his arms and be me as he has known me and knows me deeply- when others may only see the past 4 years of sever disease.

This trip was a reminder of everything I am, all that we have been through and all that we will continue to go through— with GRIT & GRACE & GOD.

I accept all of this. I don't have to love all of it but I accept where we are in this moment. Here we are. It's fucked up but ok.

| 40 |

Discussing a GoFundMe Again

It was early in 2024 that Raff discovered a glimmer of hope at a cancer treatment center in Scottsdale, AZ. Undaunted by the distance, we quickly traveled there for a consultation, and were immediately encouraged by the friendly woman across the desk who told us that they would be happy to put together a treatment plan. She presented us with some numbers. All together, with travel, lodging, food, and treatment, it would cost around $200,000 and take 12-14 weeks.

There was a long awkward pause.

Then she continued, "Are you going to pursue this?" If so, they wanted a blood test now. Right then. As in, before we left. Oh, and by the way, the blood test was another $2000. Cash up front. I think my mind was still stuck on $200,000 and 14 weeks. As I tried to wrap my head around those numbers, I tried to not let on that we had zero dollars. But I looked at Raff, and she looked at me. It was one of those unspoken moments. Eye to eye. Soulmate to soulmate that said it all. Yes, we would do it. A step of faith. We both knew we didn't have $200,000, and that we would have to scrape up the $2000 for the blood test. But we said, yes. The $2000 was just the tip of an enormous iceberg. The treatment center policy was simply pay to play. If we didn't pay upfront, we didn't get treated. Just. That. Simple.

I knew why they wanted us back immediately. Raff was losing ground. I could see it but didn't speak of it. There was so much I didn't say out loud. She was so fragile. Clinging to hope. The friendly woman at the desk had said immediately. What was immediately? Now? In an hour? Maybe tomorrow? Three days? Was that still immediately? My mind was racing as we headed back home with our empty pockets, to our empty bank accounts, and to a mailbox stuffed with unpaid bills. Terrified. How to make this work? Where were we getting $200,000 immediately? I kept thinking, *Lord, please don't make me ask people to contribute again.* I needed time to think. To figure it out. Time for all the things. I gave myself 10 days. Ten days to pull it all together. To find the cash, the housing, and the transportation. There was so much that needed to be done.

Raff and I discussed over and over how we could possibly make any of this work. We had to ask. We prayed about it, and prayed about it, and prayed about it.

Once the initial shock of the cost subsided a bit, the reality of the distance came into focus. Eleven hundred miles. Impossible to travel back and forth as we did to Tulsa and Atlanta. Raff had been bedridden for nearly a year, it would be impossible for her to sit in a vehicle for an 1100-mile trip. It would be excruciating for her. Impossible to endure. We would have to somehow get to Scottsdale and stay put for the entire 14 weeks. She had to lie face down.100% of the time going to Scottsdale, she had to lay face down because of the wounds and the pain. We need housing, too. Not just for Raff, but also for the girls and me. Family of four. Did I mention it was spring training season in Scottsdale? The cost of housing in Scottsdale was at a premium. More funds. Then, we had to weather the 1100-mile trip back. How do we pull that off? I had 10 days to figure it out. The clock was ticking.

As big as those obstacles were, I was learning that I had an underlying obstacle that created problems for me across the board. It quietly seeped in at every turn. That obstacle was my own pride. I don't know where it started but there was a false pretense, a sense that I had control. Not in a control freak kind of way, but in a capable way. I did this, I did that, I was capable, on and on and on. Trophies and BS. But when actually presented with a scenario that is clearly out of control, no ability, no answers, no means, it was all on the line, everything was at stake, what then? Here was what I did. I walked out into the silent night. Under a full moon in the night sky. I stood and stared up, then closed my eyes and pleaded, "Lord, I can show up for my family every single day, but I need your help financially." I had realized that I couldn't move this mountain alone. And, I had to move past the shame of asking. Step out of my way. Lay the pride aside and bare my soul. Tell the story. Share all her pain and suffering. Be painfully transparent about our limitations and need for help. Painfully honest. Ask again. It was our third GoFundMe.

We raised money for five years to cover treatment. But, after the first GoFundMe, where people contributed ALOT, it was extremely difficult to go back and ask again. It was against every fiber in me. That initial GoFundMe was set up when we were living on the ranch. I was physically exhausted all the time from managing cattle and doing all the ranch things. Her tumor got HUGE very quickly, and was horrifying. An oozing, gaping wound on her hip. We had to make a drastic move and Tulsa proved to be our choice. It would cost a fortune, I was barely making enough for us to eat, and our very dear friend created the GoFundMe for our family. That moment was laden with tremendous emotion. I knew we needed help, but I felt ashamed for asking, and I know Raff felt all kinds of fear and many other emotions, too.

Now, we had to ask again. Another frog to swallow. At this point I didn't think I had any pride left. Another GoFundMe? Really? How could we ask again? How do we even word something like that? People were going to think this was some kind of joke. I was keenly aware and so appreciative that all those donors dug deep the first time. We can't keep asking people for money. My brain was attacking me, and it was winning. How could we ask for more? Would anyone consider donating? And, what if no one did? What then? We had no idea what to even expect. I just wanted to crawl in a hole and hide, never to show my face.

The trickle of funds into that third GoFundMe had turned into a steady stream. Adding up. But would it be enough? At least enough to get started? Maybe cover the first few critical weeks of treatment? As I sweated bullets and constantly and obsessively checked the fund total, I also focused on securing housing and transportation. Many family members and friends searched as well. Scouring our contact lists, looking for solutions. Every path seemed to lead to a dead end.

We were at T-5 days or so when Chuck messaged. Chuck? We were acquaintances in the same bible study group. The same group where I sat by the doctor who many months before gave me the blood test tip. The blood test Raff literally had been searching the world for. Chuck typically joined the study each week via Zoom from his home in Scottsdale. Wait a minute. Scottsdale.

In his message, Chuck said he had shared our story with his daughters McKenna and Dakota, and they were adamant about helping our family. He had what he called a casita, a pool house, on his property that he offered us. We could stay there throughout the entire treatment. It was small and living would be tight. But, he said their home was full of love. It was free to us if we wanted it. Yes, it was a tremendous monetary help. It was an unbelievable no brainer. We had some angels Shannon and Robby who also rented us an RV and gave us a stack of restaurant gift cards to get us out to Scottsdale. Raff could travel in an RV because she could lay on her belly in ahe bed all the way there. You know, it was unbelievable what happened once God was in the mix. How little we had to do when we had the right posture. Humility.

Discussing a GoFundMe Again

Swallowed our pride. Waved the white flag and waited on him. Albeit not always patiently. It was within 10 days after that third GoFundMe post, that we were driving to Scottsdale. Unbelievably miraculous. We received nearly all we needed. All within that 10 days.

Humble yourselves, therefore, under God's mighty hand, that he may lift you up in due time. Cast all your anxiety on him because he cares for you. 1 Peter 5:6-7

It was March of 2024. We had transportation, living arrangements, and enough funds to make a huge dent in 14 weeks of treatment, so we headed to Arizona. Driving to Scottsdale in a big, boxy RV across the vast open desert was harrowing. Crazy high cross winds beat against the side of the RV and whipped it from side to side. I was at the helm and Raff laid on a bed in the back. Big rigs and cars had pulled over and stopped on the side of the highway because of the dangerous wind conditions. My 75 mph interstate highway clip was slowed to 35 mph. At one point I was literally blown from my lane onto the shoulder. I was so tense, on the edge of breaking, nauseated, sweating, white knuckling the steering wheel, traveling across the country, afraid I was losing my wife, about to spend more money than I had ever even seen at one time, all the while thinking *I have to be the calm one leading this family of four.* And, In the midst of all this overwhelming, heart pounding urgency, my sweet seven year old in the seat beside me said something that I will never forget. Clearly unaware of the tension and urgency in the moment, in the most endearing way she says, "Papa, I love my life so much." I just laughed. What a comedic break. My life was carried by moments like that. I needed a reminder that my perspective wasn't the only one, and often wasn't actually an accurate one. My girls saved me too many times to count. Funny, I thought I was raising them. Actually, they held me together and expanded me.

In Scottsdale, we stayed our first few nights at an extended stay hotel, which had been paid for by some angels on earth back home. It was late when we arrived, we were tired, and wanted to settle in quickly. The four of us, my mom who drove a second vehicle just in case we had a problem, all of our stuff, two fish that died in transit, and plenty of emotions. The room at the extended stay was tight. A queen bed, a foldout couch and a smidge of extra floor space, barely enough for the mattress from the RV which would be the girls' bed. There was just enough room for Raff to maneuver her walker around the girls' makeshift bed to the bathroom.

At 3:00 A.M. I heard Raff freaking out in the bathroom, I jolted up out of bed and stumbled over to the door. "The tumor fell off! The tumor fell off!" she frantically whispered. I was horrified! There was blood all over the floor, we were both in complete panic. That scene throttled me to the core. After a few moments to get our bearings and assess the situation, we confirmed that she was not actively bleeding, thankfully. And to be clear, no tumor fell off. The blood on the floor was the build up caused by fewer wound care changes throughout the day. The unfortunate truth was we were forced to learn alot about wound care throughout this journey. It was hard to describe how moments like that shook the foundation of our souls. Our nerves were just fried and then this. Our girls and my mom were literally just feet away from this fiasco. They never knew a thing. We were so thankful for their deep sleep. I can't imagine the traumatic ramifications if they would have witnessed the scene. Although we went back to bed, I'm not sure we slept. How do you just carry on?

After a week in the extended stay hotel, we moved to Chuck's casita which brought an indescribable element of peace and love.

There had been so much heartache, so much struggle, but the beauty in all this was also undeniable. The love in all this was undeniable. Chuck's daughters took to our girls like older sisters, took them horseback riding, played with them, and loved them. As a man, husband, and father, I realized there were things I couldn't buy. There were worries about the kid's hearts and their safety. At Chuck's, they were loved and safe. I overflow with emotion when I think about the relief in my soul. Forever, my girls and I are changed because of the love we were shown in the months we spent in Scottsdale. It was a gift that I can never repay. All of it came out of love, and Chuck was very clear that the love between him and his daughters brought this gift into our lives. God led us to these angels on earth who offered up their safe, loving home where we weathered our terrible storm.

While Mama rests, the girls ride.
So grateful the girls have a safe place to explore their love for horses with a rodeo babe to guide them.

| 41 |

She Loved Denim

I want to tell you all about the WEEK 1 of healing in AZ but first I needed to share a picture of myself... wearing jeans. You might ask yourself, "What is so important about a picture of Raffi wearing jeans?"
Well, it has been over a year, like WAY over a year since I have been able to wear jeans. I could not even wear my baggy jeans.

Monday after Chemo, I found a pair of jeans that fit. Today after my two days of deep deep rest and at least 24 hours of sweet sweet sleep. I put on said denim beauties, put my pink happy shirt on and rode off to my receive my IVs.

Thank You, Cancer

Today is a BIG day.

I can't wait to share more stories I have experienced. I will share some clinical stuff but it's the people here alongside the medical plans that getcha.

| 42 |

The Salt River

There was a river outside of Scottsdale called the Salt River. It was an absolute oasis in the middle of a cactus filled desert. It was the home to a magnificent herd of wild horses. We went down to the river as much as we could. We all so dearly loved the wild horses, and it was just magical to go float in the river. The cold water running over your body, tubers floating by, and magnificent rock formations juxtaposed against the beautiful sky. It was idyllic to say the least. There were trips where the wildflowers were blooming everywhere, the rolling rock terrain was blanketed in yellow magnificence. It was a dream, and we were surrounded by it. The song *Wildflowers and Wild Horses* by Lainey Wilson was our anthem for more reasons than just the obvious, but it felt like we were in the music video every time we went to that river.

Raff loved the moving water. We would talk about our dreams, and what we were going to do after she healed. She would lay there, on her belly, on the rocky bank of this magnificent river and just bask in the warmth of the sunshine. She was still not able to submerge herself in the water due to the open tumor wounds. She yearned to be in the water, so she stood in the rolling rapids and washed her hair in the pristine water. It was a silent, ever-present heartbreak to watch her stand there in the water unable to fully submerge herself because of the cursed cancer. It made me furious, and also guttingly sad for her suffering yet there was beauty in these moments.

"Take me to the river, drop me in the water."

- **wild mustangs**
- **wash hair in river**
- **made it through long drive**
- **in awe of my surroundings**
- **together with family + mother**

This is hard but life is absolutely beautiful.

Relocating our family to a new city for four months was a very lonely experience. Each day we would take Raff to the treatment center 30 minutes away, then the girls and I would spend a few hours in town. Later, we would pick up Mama and take her a fresh matcha which she loved, and then we would head back to the house. If Raff had some energy we would grab lunch somewhere in town, before heading home. This was more or less our rhythm for these months.

It was hard to get acquainted with anyone and even relate to anyone when this was our routine and reality. We just weren't doing normal things that young families do. We were excited when Raff met a wonderful young mother at the treatment center. They had a lot in common; both were patients, although with very different health issues, and both were married with two children. The two developed a mutual friendship and we were even invited to dinner at their home. I admit I was skeptical when Raff first told me about the invitation. In my mind, I thought, *Oh no. I hope this isn't a long afternoon where I'm forced to endure some awkward social scene where I have nothing in common with these people and I can't wait to escape.* But, I could not have been more off.

These beautiful humans became dear friends almost immediately, authentic friendships from that first meal together. Raff grew very close with her new friend, and I developed a strong, mutual friendship with the husband and found someone that I could relate to. Our lives were very similar as we had burned the ships, so to speak, to pursue treatment in Scottsdale. Both of our families had gone all in, left our homes, jobs, communities, and everything on this path. Maybe on the outside we appeared put together-ish. But, we were all quivering in the wind of our respective storms. We could all just relate, without any words being said. I was so grateful that we crossed paths.

There was another dimension to this friendship. Deep down, I was struggling to be useful. I had committed myself to my family and to helping find Raff a cure. But I also had a longing to be useful, bread-winner type useful, and to somehow feel as though I was making more of a contribution. Because I had spent over a decade in the fitness business, my eyes lit up when this new friend and I spoke of our need to start taking care of ourselves, including our health. As a natural offshoot of these discussions, he hired me to begin a training regiment. I actually began to make some money. I felt so blessed to receive an answer to my deep longing during that time of absolute struggle.

Our two families shared meals, we shared our struggles, we shared our hearts. Our girls had good friends that they could relate to about all of this strangeness in their lives. The magnificent puzzle pieces all fit together. Our new friends were Jewish and we were honored when they invited us to share Shabbat with them. We talked about our beliefs, our childhoods, and so many things. The depth of our friendship was profound. The soul-level connection was born out of a moment of shared struggle. Both wives were in constant fear for their lives and both husbands were fighting with everything we had to hold our families together. We found lifelong friends. When I think of the moment we had to say goodbye to this dear family, I choke up. We all cried. All eight of us. As we parted ways, he and I made eye contact. A knowing look. Was this the last time our wives would see each other? Remembering that moment, I'm shattered over and over again. Because it was just that, the last time.

| 43 |

Crash Cart

The thought of having a foreign object inserted into my body has always freaked me out.

I've had a PIC line in my arm before to administer chemo in the past. It was a terrible experience inserting it into my arm but the scar is small and it got the job done at the time.

This time around, the thought of a perma-catheter or port weighed so heavy on me. More than just the physical aspect, it was a tangible "start" to treatment. It was a "oh shit, this is happening". It was a grab at another part of my body.

I love my collar bones. I think there is something so beautiful about collar bones and the chest. There has been so much change in this body, mostly involuntary and the thought of another dig at this place, my collar bones- just felt shitty.

Thank You, Cancer

The night before the procedure, I stood in front of the mirror admiring my chest and beginning to face the fact that there would be scars there too. My body wont look the same after tomorrow. Then I busted up laughing. Laughed out loud, at myself.

Our bodies are changing and regenerating constantly. You take a poop and your body will never be the same again.

You get a tattoo and your body will never be the same again. Your cells are constantly regenerating and shedding. You can go on and on—- obviously it's a little different — these scars and the ways they get here, on our bodies. but also, it's fine— and what stories to tell.

The treatment protocol in Scottsdale was tailored to Raff. That was the number one benefit of going to Arizona for treatment. The laws offered much more specialized care, and at this point it was clear that the blanket treatment protocols that were being used elsewhere had not been effective. In our minds they were all part of a sick-care model, and no one was trying to cure this beast we were fighting, we were just another payment coming in. I was not able to be with Raff when she had her treatments. We had been through all kinds of settings, I had even sat through eight-hour-long IV's with her. Because her cancer care started during COVID, I couldn't even walk into the hospital with her. So we were used to this arrangement.

We had many people come one at a time and stay a week with us just to have time with Raff. It was always fun to have family around, particularly as we dealt with cancer treatment. It was a very welcome change from our normal schedule. So it was her mom's week and I almost lost my sh*t. The girls and I had stayed at the pool at her mom's hotel while Raff and her mom went to the treatment center. Afterwards, when we were together, I overheard Raff mention something about a crash cart. I immediately stopped her and asked what she was saying. Come to find out, the day before Raff had completely stopped breathing, and she needed a crash cart. Now, this was at least 30 hours after it happened that I was finding out. I was shaken beyond belief.

I am not a doctor, nor am I an insurance company, but this was my understanding. Just do your own research. Apparently, in some settings, the chemotherapy dosage that is given is what was administered in a trial. This is done because that dosage is what the insurance companies have agreed to cover. But in our case, insurance was not part of the game. We were on a cash basis, and as I mentioned we were in a state that had more flexible laws. They tailored Raff's treatment exactly to her tolerance which was just 10% of the approved dosage. After hearing about the crash cart scenario, I was very thankful we chose the setting we did. But also, what would happen in the event that she was given the full dose? Does that just get written off to a legal loophole? This was a shocking reality of our sick-care system. Another reason to do your research, and always keep looking. After that week, they changed her treatment regimen by using an alternate drug and she safely received 10 or more doses of chemotherapy at the correct level. This was so unsettling to me.

After so many years of undergoing treatment, I think I had forgotten how potent these drugs are and how fragile life is. We had become numb to inputs, numb to circumstances. We unknowingly shielded ourselves from the ferocity of reality, we were just so desperate. The struggle in these years was intense.

I want to stay present and celebrate all the positive changes, all the healing that is happening. I treat it like a full time job where I just have to show up, get plugged in, and then go home. As I heal, as all this positive momentum of physical regeneration happens— it can be hard to stay focused.

The "what happens when..." gets in the way of "look what's happening now!".

I don't worry about the past as much as I used to. I would lay in bed and comb over every little detail and over analyze my past.

Thank You, Cancer

I've done enough of that and now that I'm here - so much of the past has been put to bed with recognition of how it has impacted my current situation.
I let it go.

The "what happens when/if..." is trying to take hold but I breathe and set it aside. I go over all the positive changes happening in my body, my heart— I go over the good the girls experience, my husband's love and presence, I recite the bites of scripture I can remember. I shush the "what happens when..." it's not happening now so sssshhhhhh.

I'm busy healing.

It has been almost a year since I have been able to walk upright, for a significant distance other than to the car or around the house. It has been almost a year since l have engaged these muscles that hold the memory of all my sprints, all my lifts, the cadence of my walk, the squats, and the muscle twitches of 30+ years past.

This past week, without thinking much of it- I told Danny,

"Nah" as we did the usual drop off at he center. He walked to the back of the car to get my roller walker but I was late and wanted to get going with therapies. So, I said no to the roller without much thought. I walked into the center and heard, "RAFFI!!", "Raffi, no walker!",
", claps from the other side of the room. I looked down and it hit me that I walked into the center without the walker, without pain. Just mozied on in.

I am walking tall, moving slow and steady.

I am walking tall.

Our time in Scottsdale was divided. There was a first run of treatment and then a second. In the middle there was a procedure that we believed would be very helpful that was more of an elective, but we were pretty sure it would be part of the plan. This was called the Chemo Immuno Precision Injections (CIPI), a very pricey specialized treatment where tumors are directly injected and destroyed. We had gone round and round about the positives and negatives of the CIPI procedure. On the way in, everything we heard from the team was positive. Even when we talked about weighing the cost vs more weeks of general treatment, the choice was still CIPI. So when it was time for the procedure, I got a phone call as I was driving with our girls. The treatment center needed to debit $15,000 from our account that day. I cleared the balance as I tried not to veer off the road. Then, almost immediately, I got another call. They needed to debit another $15,000 from our account. In three blocks, $30,000 was torched. This was a very surreal moment. The storm of emotion coupled with gratitude which coursed through my body in the car at that time was INSANE. I was rattled but at the same time comforted that we had a tremendous group of humans from all over the planet that generously supported us through all of this. These funds were all a gift from God through them, literally angels that walked on earth. On my own I stood no chance. This was a front row moment to His story that I cannot go without telling.

They sold property and possessions to give to anyone who had need. Acts 2:45

Instead of postponing this procedure as I did my diagnosis— I am thanking God that I have a team that will carry me through with love, empathy and delicate hands to hold my body in vulnerable positions as we assist these tumors in breaking down.

I will breathe through it.
I will speak up when I need to.
I will let myself cry as I need to.
I will pray with my team, OUTLOUD as much as I need to.
I will pause if I need to.

Sexual, vaginal trauma will not have a hold on me. It will not have a hold on my life anymore.
It has been over 3 1/2 years since I was diagnosed. Diagnosed much later than I needed to be, with spread to the lymph nodes that may not have happened if had been able to address my past.
This week I am undergoing a procedure called CIPI (Chemo Immune Precision Injections). A micro catheter will guide medications such as chemo, along with natural substances such as baking soda into the tumor. Due to the location of the tumors and my specific situation, I will be positioned to access tumors in mom pelvis both internally and externally.

It has taken me a few weeks to wrap my head around the procedure. We met with the doctor and nurse, went through scans, procedures, medications, the whole thing. I had expected to feel nauseous, clamp up and feel my body switch into fight or flight mode. To my surprise, and relief -- I let myself cry and expressed my concerns, the reason behind them and was able to advocate for myself. We decided it was best that I would be fully sedated.

The nurse assured me that they would not touch me or prep me until I was fully sedated. The doctor continued to ask if there was anything else I felt I needed. We continued to talk things through as I needed, with the doctor present and fully engaged in the conversation to meet my needs.

I wasn't triggered or filled with fear when I left the meeting. I don't feel fear now, two days away from the procedure. My body, mind, heart and soul are in a different place than they were years ago- how could they not be? I don't play the traumas in my mind over and over anymore. I don't over analyze them. It has taken me almost 3 1/2 years to stop ruminating to surrender it all and let God. I have connected all the dots I need to in order to move forward, to allow these tumors to be decimated and dissolved.

Part 3 :: The days before I cried a decent amount. It wasn't because I was dreading the procedure or that I was scared. There was a sadness that needed to be expressed. It felt like another moment of vulnerability as I would mostly be passed out while my body bare is exposed. The places that you protect, laid out on the CT scan bed. This was going to be different. I felt the Lord calm my spirit and put the word "checkpoint" on my heart.

This time, through tears, I spoke with each person on my team as they checked in, I advocated for myself. Before I was rolled into the room, my pregnant nurse came to my side and checked in with me. With tears in her eyes, she shared that between her pregnancies she had experienced extensive testing after a cancer scare. I felt seen, as a woman, a mother, and a wife rather than a scared or sad patient.

After I hopped onto the bed of the CT scanner, laid on my belly with my hands above my head and imagined I was at the beach in the sunshine.

As I woke up the doctor came over and gave his report of the procedure. The tumors were much smaller than expected. Four points on my butt cheeks made for the catheter to reach my lymph nodes. Those points were enough to reach the vaginal areas of concern as well.

According to the doctor it was a challenging procedure but in the best way; "a good problem to have" he shared. Nothing I imagined happened. What happened was that I felt cared for regardless of what was going to happen during the procedure. I felt compassion and respect for the procedure as well as for myself as the patient. What I felt was a sense of gratitude, a sense of peace that the page was truly turning in this chapter.

A checkpoint.

What I felt was healing.

We had some time between treatments so we decided to head to a place that feels like heaven on earth, Sedona, AZ. Red rock formations jut up out of the earth in the most majestic formations. Ice cold rivers running through the canyons. The majesty of God's creation is just everywhere. My words don't do justice to this magnificent oasis. Chapel of the Holy Cross is built into the rock majesty, and was first on our list to visit. The views are breathtaking, His presence is breathtaking, the whole trip was such a blessing.

We tried an update in real time!

Update: i received the results of a negative biopsy
• Sa. It
led to a couple of days of silence and anger, and joy and so so many feelings I am still working through.
There is still so much healing that needs to happen. As much as I already knew that and know the reality of our situation I wanted life to pause for a moment. For so many reasons I expected ballon's to drop, a dance party to happen and for real life to just pause.

Sedona, with majestic rocks and incredible views filled me up with it's wonder.

We're still healing and dealing but with the best news in hand and a HUGE step in the right direction.

I am headed out of AZ and heading home in a few weeks. My greatest struggle is my mental space and staying out of fear as I enter the home, the space I was so so sick for so long.

I'm not scared of cancer progressing. I feel healed in a way that I can't quite put into words. There is a lot that I can't quite put into words as I process these past few months.
In this transition home, as we have started making plans and switching my care — it is my mind and the words that I speak/think over these cells that are working so hard to keep me moving, healing and functioning as optimal as possible in this moment and every moment to come.

Maybe it will be a helpful reminder to others who are healing. The power of our minds, our thoughts, our heart posture. It all matters. I know for myself in this moment, it is something I am working on and I hope you will join.

Your cells are listening, what will you speak/think into them?

| 44 |

Evidence of Disease

Life update :: we received so much clarity today in our appt. I've been struggling the past two weeks with a huge question mark of concern. Figured out what is causing all the startling pain and have a solution, thank God!

Circulating tumor cell marker went down! I need it to be 0. It has been dropping and thankfully is continuing to drop! Woop woop. Heading out of Arizona tomorrow (let me wipe the sweat off my brow)
So pretty and so hot.

We're going home with "evidence of disease" as a few parting words. It leaves me slightly unsettled, honestly. This journey has wreaked havoc on my body. I don't understand it but I believe in it's healing power, and God's healing power. The emotions that have passed through me range widely. It has changed me in ways I never could have expected or prepared for. No one talks about the "aftermath". The repair of heart, mind, soul, and body.

I'm excited to get home and grateful to have time and space between AZ and KC to begin processing these four months. We are all ready to be home.

S L O W days.
I'm not sure if I'm ready to be back, but we're back home for a couple of weeks. Friendships and nature holding us together while we navigate life now. PETscan is soon.

Concern of this and that looming — the team we hoped for feeling so distant and no longer a fit. We've grown so much and don't quite know where we fit yet. Still processing so much, sleep so needed, staying out of our heads and in our faith, in nature, in movement seems to be the only thing getting us through at the moment.

healing happens here healing happens here

| 45 |

Back, But Not Home

After four months in the Arizona desert, we headed back home. We had a nagging feeling that we really didn't want to go back, but that was our house at the moment, and that was where all of our stuff was. So to Kansas City we went. With all the months that we had been gone, and throughout this five-year journey, we never felt like we had a home town. Our home was always each other, and with all of our travel we felt kind of lost at the moment.

During the last weeks of our time in Scottsdale, the tumors seemed to be gaining ground. I'm really not sure what flipped the switch and seemed to reverse all the ground we had covered, but the backslide was very real. Almost immediately after we arrived in Kansas City, I could tell Raff did not want to be there. There was something about going back to the place where she laid for two years, where she thought she was dying. The space really weighed heavily on her.

Her mental space was very important and I could see those days were costing her. She was descending into a dark space, and it affected her more and more by the day. I knew I had to get her out of that house. Granted, we were able to see friends who we hadn't seen in months which was really nice for all of us, but as energetic beings, more or less collections of energy, the overall energy in our home was declining. We could feel it. Just as you feel the temperature, it was that obvious. We knew it was time to go. So we set our sights on Austin, TX, to visit her sister and just endured the days until it was time to leave. Raff said just wanted to sleep until we left for Texas.

Weeks before, Raff told me something that caused me to reconsider our path. She told me that she regretted not raising our daughters with their little cousins. That she regretted not being near her brother and sister, that all she really wanted was to be near her family. So, if we moved, we would have to choose, the Chicago area where her brother lived or the Austin area where her sister lived. Since Raff didn't like the cold anymore because she had so much scar tissue, Austin made the most sense.

We packed our stuff, jumped in the car, and headed south on Interstate 35 toward Texas. We had talked about moving to Austin many times in the past months, so in my mind it was a done deal, especially after the experience of coming home. But, the two of us hadn't officially discussed it, and we knew the girls were going to be very resistant.

We arrived in mid-July to plenty of heat, but energetically we could feel the difference. It was a welcome change for all of us. We landed at her sister's apartment which seemed the perfect spot to get our feet wet in possibly our new home town. During the first few weeks the four of us had daily coffee dates, or visited a park or one of Austin's famous water features. Watching Raff and her sister brought me great joy. They shared a special bond, as many sisters do, but watching them laugh and be together, especially in this moment was truly a gift. Our hearts were so happy. Despite all the heartache, I believe that move was the best choice we had. Of course every decision was pivotal and meant trade offs, but, to me, none of them outweighed the importance of this move.

A few weeks into our so-called *visit* to Austin, Raff made it clear she didn't want to go back to Kansas City. It wasn't a surprise, I could see it coming. So it was settled, we were moving to Austin; we just had to break the news to the girls. Our decision was met with some resentment and big emotions, but in the end, the girls agreed that finding care for Mama, and being with her family was the most important thing. I can't tell you that making decisions as a unit was easy, because it was not, nor was weathering the storm easier with more humans; but I can tell you I would not do it any other way. Our girls are shockingly resilient, they have emotional IQs that are insane, and they saved me many days. This is because we walked that path together.

Getting care lined up in Austin proved to be harder than we thought; it was a trip to the emergency room that fast-forwarded us into the system. It was August of 2024, roughly three months since our last treatment in Scottsdale and we knew Raff needed medical attention. The tumor load had been increasing and her life signs were decreasing. I had been calling around and it was clear that if we could even get in to see a doctor, we could be many months away from any sort of treatment. Months that we didn't have.

The initial energy and excitement from the change of scenery had worn off, and as we spent more weeks in the apartment, Raff was getting out of bed less and less. Walking became nearly impossible. She was unable to raise her feet over the edge of the tub to get in to clean herself. She was in bed 24/7, she maybe got up about once every 7-10 days or so, but even this was costly on her physically. Her general spirit was diminishing.

Now, I had been with her every day for five years and I think it was sometimes hard for me to see the forest for the trees. It was her sister who called me and suggested that she go to the emergency room.

The moment she said it, I knew she was right, and could see it! I totally agreed. Her condition was just a whisper above needing an ambulance.

The apartment was on an upper floor about 75 yards from the elevator, then there was another 30 yards or so across the parking lot to the car. Raff could barely walk 10 steps. The weakness in her body was severe, she would get incredibly winded and have to stop for a breather about every 10 steps. I couldn't carry her due to the tumor locations. They were on the outside of her body. If she sat on a saddle, she had tumors everywhere that her body made contact with the saddle; and when touched they would bleed, and bleed A LOT. That had to be the worst and most cruel place for a woman to have such wounds. She was so proud to be a mother, and was a mother to so many in so many ways. The fact that she was attacked there, like that. The horror was indescribable. She couldn't sit on her tumor-covered bottom, a wheelchair was out, we had no choice but to slowly walk.

I vividly recall the walk to the car, and it makes me break out in a sweat. With her walker, we started down the hall. It took us forever. We stopped for breaks many times. I told her I was going to call the ambulance at least twice, but she kept on. She had reserves of strength that I could not believe. There was just no way to make this part easier, we had to walk it out. Between the tears, the shaking legs, the exhausted breathing, and me freaking out inside and trying to keep my composure, we made it to the elevator. *At least a moment to rest*, I thought. But after we got there and the elevator door opened she said she couldn't continue. Now we are too far out to stop, and she can't just lay down in the hall, we had to continue. We were both at the end of our ropes, but somehow she found more strength, on her quivering legs and with tear-filled eyes she was able to make it to the car.

But we were far from done. She had to get into the car. She had just made that impossible marathon walk, she was totally fatigued, and she was out of breath like she just climbed a mountain. Any inadvertent bump or contact with the tumors as she got into the car would open a floodgate of profuse bleeding. Those tumors would erupt at the slightest pressure, they couldn't even be lightly brushed with a hand. Yet, somehow she managed to get in. I don't know where she got the strength to strategically maneuver herself into the front seat but she did. She was able to get her back on the seat and put her feet up on the dashboard to keep her weight off the giant tumor. Unbelievable. It was a testament to a well of strength many of us may never know.

The emergency waiting room was full when we got to the hospital, full of people who had been there for a good while by the looks of their faces. I had left Raff in the car to go in and explain our situation. By the grace of God, they immediately brought out a gurney where she could lie on her belly and took us right back.

That hospital visit was the first of a few hospital stays we had coming up. I believe we were there for six days. She was having a host of issues. The most pressing was that of calcium levels in her blood. The tumor load made her parathyroid produce a hormone that pulled calcium into her bloodstream. This was the crux of her recent problems. Hypercalcemia causes heart issues, it also causes neurological issues. She was having trouble finding words, she couldn't remember things, she was very fatigued. These are all issues because of this calcium thing. We had been trying another round of immunotherapy hoping to combat the tumor growth. At this point I believe we had completed two treatments but we were losing ground to the tumors. So the new battle was to get the calcium down. Within a few days with plenty of meds and a few transfusions, the calcium was under control. We were so relieved, but the reality was that we were just back to where we started the week before. The tumors were still raging, continually pulling calcium back into the blood.

A message popped up out of nowhere that was sent by a girl who went to my high school. I didn't know her, we weren't even in the same class but she knew about our story. Renee had lost her husband to cancer two years before while she was nursing the last of their six children. She wanted us to know that they had a river house about an hour south of us, and they would love to have us stay there for a week whenever we were able. Right away we made plans to go in early October.

During our stay at the river house, the girls and I took a drive just to see the river. Raff stayed back resting which was her MO these months. The girls and I just meandered along River Road next to the beautiful Guadalupe River that rolls through Gruene, TX. As we searched for a place to jump in, we realized that outfitters buy up all the shoreline, so there was really no place to go take a dip unless you paid for a day pass. We found an outfitter and paid the day rate. I took a dirt parking lot as far as I could and then we walked. We were there in the offseason thankfully, so we basically had the place to ourselves.

We found the most beautiful spot. It was like nature collided there to produce crystal clear rolling rapids, huge cypress trees that had moss hanging like feathers, birch trees on the other side nestled against a meadow, and pools teeming with little fish. The rocks were worn beautifully and the exposed roots of the trees created endless nooks for sitting. There was a perch of rocks right in the middle, from which we were able to gaze down into the storybook view and listen to the birds as the sun beamed through the cypress. It was literally a dream. I felt as if God wanted us to bring her there. We couldn't wait to get back and tell Mama about our crazy find.

It was the very next day, we were on our way to the river with Mama and her dear friend Maria who was in town. Incredibly, between her walker and some help from our crew, we traversed the rocky 50 yards or so from the car to the rock outcropping in storybook land. She had spent all her time for months sleeping, reading, or looking at the wall in front of her as she laid on her belly. And, today she was there in that storybook. We brought cushions for her to lay on and enjoy the afternoon.

Back, But Not Home

We were able to get her into the water, and she felt the little fish nibbling on her legs and toes. We got some laughs in. These laughs and smiles were treasures. She washed her hair in the cold river, which was one of her favorite things to do. She loved moving water. It was in her soul. She craved it like nothing else. I cannot fathom how this felt to her, but the joy I felt was overwhelming, and to be honest, it still is.

That day was Magic.

Little did any of us know, this would be her last adventure. From this point forward, she was homebound, except for a few more harrowing trips to the doctor. In this final year, the intensity moved far beyond a fever pitch. But while we were down at the river house, God was working behind the scenes bringing us another absolute miracle.

We had been looking to get a house in Austin basically since we'd arrived. Her sister's apartment was our landing pad, but not a forever solution and we all knew it. But here's the hitch, the first thing a landlord asks for is proof of employment, for obvious reasons. I didn't have proof of recent employment. I had been unemployed and taking care of my family for 13 months; ever since I got fired from my last employer. Obviously, we had been fundraising for the past five years, and speaking from a dollars and cents perspective, we could have paid for a home. But, that doesn't count as employment. There was also the school puzzle that had to be figured out. Austin had neighborhood schooling, so if you lived next to a trash school, that was what you got. School was a priority as Raff was a teacher by trade and one of the best I might add. So there was definitely pressure to find a home in the right location.

I found a beautiful home that met our key requirement. It was in a neighborhood right behind a great school. It was both for sale and for rent. I called the realtor on a Friday and told her we wanted it, and we were ready for an immediate move in. However, just the day before the owner had placed an extension on a sale contract. The offer was below asking price but the buyer still had four days, nothing could be decided until the term ended. Heartbroken, I selfishly hoped the offer would fall through. In spite of the contract, I wrote a very heartfelt letter about our situation being as blunt and honest as I possibly could, which led to a great phone conversation with the owner. I remember that I was sitting out in the back of the river house overlooking a cattle ranch when he told me they would accept our offer to rent. BUT..... in the State of Texas, the extension had to be honored, and IF the buyer still wanted the house it was theirs. I was thrilled and horrified.

It was very obvious that we were nearing Raff's last season. We had the two kids, who needed school, we moved 700 miles to be with her family, we were all in, and the pressure was paralyzing. We had until Tuesday at 5 o'clock before we would know. I tried to keep my brain occupied but the days were torture. But, Tuesday finally came. I had messaged the realtor so many times hoping for some good news. Crickets. I must have checked my phone 900 times that day. I felt like I was going to burst. As the afternoon drew on, I busied myself with a quick run to the store and to grab some gas. Unexpectedly, and as I stood there by the car in the Texas evening sun filling up the tank, my phone rang. It was the owner. But it was 4:17, not 5 o'clock yet. My heart stopped. I was mortified. My finger shook as I went to answer. He told me that the buyer had cancelled their offer and the house was ours. Overcome with relief, tears burst from my eyes. I was standing at the gas station sobbing, so full of gratitude at what just transpired. I stood there in the sunlight and thanked God for what He had done.

I rushed to the store and then back to the river house, where the three girls were waiting. I didn't say anything just waited until we were all in the same room then casually prefaced a sentence with, "Well, since we got the house." Raff turned to me with tears streaming down her face. We all hugged. Another HUGE moment. We all thanked God for that moment. The thought that this house might be our last as a family of four never crossed my mind. We just desperately needed a home to call our own and against all odds, we had one.

Every good and perfect gift is from above, coming down from the Father of the heavenly lights, who does not change like shifting shadows. James 1:17

About four weeks later we returned to the ER repeating the whole grueling walk-to-the-car fiasco again. By God's grace we made it. We had set out only to get an infusion, but they required that she go to the

ER first because her low calcium levels were now considered an oncological emergency. Raff was not allowed to receive the infusion. She was literally lying on a bench in the hallway outside of the treatment center, too weak to move, too weak for treatment; and we were told that in spite of her herculean effort to get there she was not allowed the infusion. We were filled with heartbreak and panic, just crushed.

Now here was a not so funny BS insurance story. We were at the infusion center, across the street from the hospital. Raff was unable to walk, unable to sit in a wheelchair, and I couldn't carry her; yet they insisted she go to the ER first. The Emergency Medical Service [EMS] had to take her, it was just three turns around the block, they charged us $1000, and the doctors had to admit her, all before she could get the infusion. It was amazing how difficult these moments were, and then there's all of that. By the way, the EMS guys were great.

Anyway, back to the ER. It was the same calcium game and she was admitted again. Everything is harder. She was barely able to get in and out of bed. I won't go into all the problems we dealt with, the constipation, bleeding, wound care, doctors and nurses visiting all throughout the nights, lack of sleep, constant needle pricks, rolling veins, crying, etc. Those days were terrible. She didn't feel comfortable going to the bathroom with anyone but me. Not a complaint as I signed up for this and would rather be nowhere than by her side.

After another exhausting hospital stay of four or five days, we returned home. It seemed like we kept repeating the same lap around a treacherous and exhausting track to never get anywhere, and Raff showed the fatigue. I couldn't imagine how this could happen again. I couldn't imagine how we could do another trip to the hospital after the last time. When I said we barely made it home, I cannot stress to you how fine the line was between a successful trip and complete disaster.

| 46 |

"When I'm all they have, they'll have all of me."

Our 10th anniversary was October 11, 2024, and we moved into our new house the week after. To be real honest as this date drew closer, I was just praying that Raff would make it long enough for us to celebrate together. Years back we talked about getting remarried on our 10th anniversary. It's crazy where life goes. We were both so exhausted just by the logistics of our life our *so-called celebration* ended up being just a kiss and sort of a hug. There was heartbreak all over in this story, but we really felt it when our reality was so far from where we thought it would be.

I'll paint a canvas of our days. Everything revolved around wound care, it had been at an all time high for months now. We were tipping the scales at about $40 per day on wound care supplies. The holes in the financial boat were nearly impossible to fill. She had to go to the bathroom, maybe five or six times in a 24-hour period, and I would help her get there. I would slowly walk with her down the short hall.

I would walk backwards as we held each other's elbows and shuffled our way. There was no using the toilet. I would help her into the tub by lifting her calf so she could get one foot in the tub, then I lifted the other. As she stood in the tub, the soiled bandaging was removed and tossed away, then she took care of everything else, standing under the shower. She was there for 15-45 minutes each time, then I helped her out. We cleaned and re-bandaged the tumors using up to six non-stick 8" by 10" gauze pads each time, then I shuffled her back to bed. There, I slowly lifted each leg, one at a time to get her onto the bed. She just did not have the muscle strength to move her body. Everything else fit in between the bathroom trips; cooking, cleaning, and all the activities that eight and nine year olds bring into the picture including homeschooling.

There were so many details to this horror which created sights I couldn't unsee. Maybe like those haunting post traumatic stress disorder [PTSD] memories. I do want to share one scenario to help illustrate the magnitude of the suffering she so gracefully endured. There were two distinct moments of uncontrolled bleeding, like "Hey, Babe! Come in here!" Tumors are wildly vascular, meaning gobs and gobs of blood vessels; once they started to bleed, the blood came fast. So, what happened when that faucet started gushing? Well, in the simplest terms, don't freak out. Simple to say, but not the easiest to do. Those moments would spring up out of nowhere.

Both times that she had uncontrollable bleeding, Raff and I were in the bathroom about to completely lose it. The steady stream of blood that shot onto the wall was terrifying. I had full scale panic as I desperately tried to keep my voice calm and my hands steady. I could only imagine what was happening in her heart and mind. But I was thankful for the calm nerves that allowed us to proceed with care and grace. In both cases, we gently bandaged the wounds, got her to bed, and with a deep sigh of relief, thanked the Lord that the bleeding stopped.

At times like those a major concern was the kids; that they would hear our distress or see something that would horrify them. They were al-

When I'm all they have, they'll have all of me

ways out and about in the house, and though they may not be close, they were always tuned in. They often knew what was happening. Raff always did a marvelous job shielding them from her eviscerating pain. They never saw the blood, the tumors, the wound care, not once in five years. I can't even wrap my head around the herculean effort it took Raff to stay infection free for the entire five years of this journey.

During those months in our new house we had a continuous stream of friends and family come to help. I was on call 24-hours a day so the relief of another human to help with the girls and household tasks was of paramount importance. It also was nice to just have another personality around, there were some very sad times during the five years, and it was easy to mentally go into a dark space.

Inside of our decision to move were so many challenges. One challenge was the girls and their friends back in Kansas City, very close friends who they were not happy to leave. To the girls, we were embarking on just another journey, and it was a challenge to get the girls' buy-in again. We all had very close friends there that made leaving sad for us as well. My mother came to help. She was here for months, she saved me, and I could not imagine making it through those months without her support. My dad drove back and forth countless times, 12 hours from Kansas to Texas. I am forever thankful to both of them.

During this time, we found a church home. My mom was staying with us and had invited the girls to go with her to church one Sunday. We thought it was a great idea, and had hopes to go as a family soon when Raff healed up and was feeling better. Having a church home was pretty important to us, we just hadn't been able to pursue it. So my mom and the girls headed off to church. A few hours later they walked in just beaming. The girls had a blast, they loved the church. Wait, wait, wait. Hold on. We had been to many, many churches in our years before this and the girls could have cared less for any of them. We were talking about big bands, coffee shops, huge kids programs, and the girls were always like EHHHH, it's ok. But this one, they loved. We had to know why. Apparently, as soon as they sat down, a little girl came up to Rue and asked her to come along to their Kids' Club. They had a ball, and the girls both still just love going to this Kids' Club. One of our biggest concerns when we moved was that the girls would lose their friends, and now they had an avenue to make new friends, and I did too. Turns out the pastor is like an old friend to me as well. God so perfectly delivered a safe space for us to build new relationships. This church home was the doorway He so eloquently led us to. What a blessing.

Jesus said, "Let the little children come to me, and do not hinder them, for the kingdom of heaven belongs to such as these." Matthew 19:14

We were well into fall. Fall in Austin seemed to arrive more slowly and the changes were more subtle than those in Kansas. Almost barely noticeable. What was noticeable though, was that we were landing the plane. The tumor was noticeably larger. I never mentioned it to Raff because I didn't want her to know that I thought we were nearing the end. We carried on through these fall days struggling to cover the cost of wound care supplies. We went through gauze pads so fast we resorted to ordering box loads from Amazon. When one of our nursing contacts saw what was happening, she referred us to palliative care. Right away, they sent out a month's worth of supplies, a gift that would have cost us well over $1000.

I made a choice in the last weeks of Raff's time with us. And just like any choice, it had consequences. We were in a triage environment. I had to make snap decisions. This decision involved the girls. For years we had a bedtime routine. Raff or I would snuggle with them in their room, maybe read a book, sing a song, and say prayers. I hadn't been there for them as much lately because I spent all my waking hours in our bedroom with Raff. So, in these last weeks, when bedtime came around, my mom and I started to tag team. She mostly covered and occasionally I would. When it was my turn, we noticed that the girls would sometimes open up and talk about their feelings and worries about Mama. My mom thought that was important, so important that she stopped me one day and told me she thought the girls could use some Papa time. I couldn't disagree, but I knew papa time would have to wait. I looked at my mom and said, "When I'm all they have, they will have all of me." For an instant we just locked eyes, knowingly. She didn't say more. We never spoke of it again.

At that moment I chose Raff, I chose to be with her for those days. I don't regret that decision. I sensed the end was near and I wasn't about to be away these last moments. I couldn't bear the thought of Raff just fading away alone. Let this be a testament to our love story. I fully trusted that I would have time to make up some ground with my girls. I also knew they were watching. Watching their parents love each other till the end. I thought that was powerful. They saw it. I'm proud of that.

On Thanksgiving Ace would not come out of her room for dinner. She was visibly upset, so I went in to talk with her. She had her head buried in her pillows for a long time. When she finally lifted her head, through her tear-filled eyes and sobbing breaths she was able to tell me that she was afraid to look at Mama. She was afraid because it made her think Mama was going to die. She didn't even want to see her because she was afraid. I was not prepared for what she said, and it broke my heart. It still brings me to tears, and causes emotional surges. It kills me to even tell the story. I gently tried to draw her out of the room and back to the table but she would not budge. I walked out of her room alone visibly shook and everyone could see it. Raff asked me what was wrong, and I had to go tell her that Ace was afraid to see her. We had some hard conversations over the years, but that one about took me out. I still feel nauseous as I write about it.

It was our sweet friend Momo that was able to finally get Ace to come out and hold Mama's hand at the table, and we were able to celebrate as a family. Honestly, this turned out to be my favorite Thanksgiving. The food was amazing, and we were together. We all were able to eat together that Thanksgiving. That night when I snuggled with Ace, she told me that her proudest moment of the day was when she held Mama's hand. Hearing her process those things was heartbreaking and heartwarming all at the same time, creating waves of emotion.

Thank You, Cancer

It was hard to tell how much time we had left with Raff. Back in September, I was unsure if she would be there for my birthday, or for our 10th anniversary in October, or for Thanksgiving. And then, she was there for Ace's eighth birthday on November 30. I was so thankful for that. I was so nervous and so broken for so long thinking she wouldn't make it, and that could leave the darkest cloud in Ace's life. But she made it! We celebrated as a family. Ace had even overcome her fear. Her fear of seeing Mama so thin and weak had subsided so that she was able to go in and talk with Mama all the time. Another gift. A tremendous gift actually. We received so many gifts. Big and small. Small things become really big things in times like these.

Our anxiety grew as we anticipated another immunotherapy appointment the first week in December. Raff's weakness drove everything. Her trips to the bathroom were down to about two or three per day. She just didn't have the wherewithal to sustain herself physically. Her walking was labored, her breathing was labored, it was all so impossible. After our last trip to the hospital, I knew there was no way she would be able to get in the car again like she had done so many times. She had to be transported on her belly or it wasn't going to happen. I had called around to see if a transportation service could make it happen, and there was nothing beyond just calling an ambulance. So I decided to make it happen myself.

We owned a Honda Element, and that may be the most versatile car I have ever seen. I built a retractable bed inside. When the back of the car was opened, the bed could slide out like a drawer, Raff could get on her belly, and I could just slide her back in. I planned it on paper, built it, and it worked flawlessly. At the hospital, a gurney could be conveniently wheeled right up next to the retractable bed, and she could slide from one to the other with a little help. Then from the gurney she could slide onto a hospital bed. It all worked so smoothly.

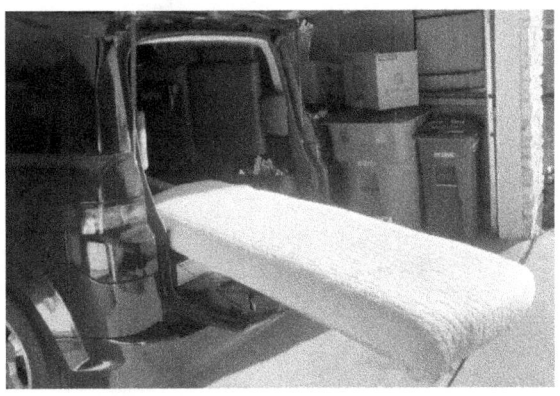

We had found out the hard way that insurance companies had strict rules about where drugs could be administered which made something that could be so simple, so difficult. We had not been allowed to have immunotherapy in a hospital room. We had tried many times. I asked and asked. Finally, on that day, I was able to work out an arrangement with the hospital to have the immunotherapy in the hospital room so we didn't have to make yet another trip to the infusion center. I'll skip all the conversations and detail, but it ended up being a 10-hour day. There was the treatment, I believe another transfusion, more drugs, and all the waiting time in between. Finally, after all that time, she was back on the gurney, then onto the custom bed, and back into the Element. We were beyond exhausted. Once at home, she laid on the bed in the car, in the garage for over an hour just due to exhaustion, and could barely make it inside. Thank goodness, Momo was there to help. I literally still can't believe it all worked out. Raff thanked me for building the retractable bed; that thank you from her meant more to me than I can ever express. I was so happy and proud that we were able to get her to the treatment without a hitch. It felt like such a victory. I had so much underlying personal worry all the time. Feeling as if I wasn't helping her, or fixing the situation. It burned in me so deep, I almost couldn't bear it.

We were hoping for a healing miracle with this last treatment, but that was not our path.

| 47 |

The H Word

The conversation we hadn't had was haunting me. For months I was haunted. Hospice was clearly the next step. If it was me, I would have made this decision, if it was my kids I would have made this decision. But it wasn't me or my kids. Raff and I discussed everything for as long as we had known each other. We decided together. I was not about to go over her head and make a decision like this without her. It was very important that we worked through whatever we needed to before deciding. But with her on and off neurological challenges, her wherewithal for laser-focused conversation was in a very small window that was only there sometimes. Also, I was concerned that if I spoke of hospice, it would break Raff's spirit. Above everything I wanted to protect her spirit, but THIS. THIS would be the epitome of breaking someone's spirit. Hospice, infamously known as the final curtain call. It was over when hospice came in. Maybe not always, but that was our impression.

As I was sitting next to her, I told her that I needed help. If she fell or something else happened, we would not have any choice but to call an ambulance, then she would have to stay in a hospital. I explained that hospice would bring everything to her, they would help, and they would make this transition easier. In her DEEP well of love for me, she agreed that I needed help, and that it was important that I got that help. It was obvious after all these years that it was taking a toll on me. In all of her pain and suffering, she held space for me. I can't tell you how blessed I felt for marrying this incredible woman. She looked past ALL of the negative stuff and yielded to me. WOW. I still lose my breath at her display of selfless love. That's Who She Was. And, this monster of a conversation that I so dreaded just unfolded so easily, as if we were talking about the weather. She made the choice to call hospice. This was my choice as well.

Hospice help arrived on a Tuesday, the bed and supplies were delivered on Wednesday, and by Thursday we had met the nurses, had all the supplies, and everything was set. She had a bit more energy that day following her immunotherapy treatment, and I was relieved to have other humans with much more medical knowledge there to help. The nurse showed me how to change the bandaging in the new bed which was so much easier. The bed caught the girls' attention and Raff in her usual thoughtful way helped ease their anxiety by demonstrating its features, giving them rides up and down which brought them smiles. Everything seemed so much easier and less tense that day, and we were actually looking forward to her first night in the new bed. It was all something to get used to, but still just another indication that the end was near.

It was 9 o'clock that night as I helped Raff walk the 20 feet or so to the bathroom from our living room couch. The girls and my mom were trying to fall asleep in their room across the hall. As we turned into the bathroom, Raff's legs completely gave out. I almost can't even write about it. Like one of those dolls that you press the bottom of and it collapses. It was just like that. So fast, I couldn't catch her. She dropped to her knees and screamed, then began to weep. Her body immediately rocked back on her heels to her butt, which is when I caught her a bit. I think she thought the tumor hit her heels, which would be terrible. The girls heard it all, it took place right outside their bedroom door. We could hear them wailing uncontrollably as my mom tried to comfort them and as I was trying to comfort Raff. I had long feared the day that she might fall. I had run so many scenarios in my head and always tried to plan for and avoid them, and here we were. It was 10 minutes of complete panic. We were all beside ourselves with panic. Slowly the panic subsided and we stopped crying, but the shock hung thick in the air.

After all that, we had another hour just to get Raff into bed. She slowly crawled the next 15-20 feet into our bedroom to the side of her bed, and I promise you, we tried everything to get her into that bed. It was maybe 18 inches off the floor. We could not do it. Her body was so weak, I tried to lift her, but her legs had no strength, she felt like a rag doll. This was so crushing. She was just panicked, as I was. I pulled the mattress off her bed onto the floor and she was able to crawl onto it, then I dragged the mattress across the floor to the foot of my bed and slept backwards to keep an eye on her. Somehow we eventually slept, but even the next morning we were still pretty shook. The nurse came early. She, Raff's mom, my mom, and I lifted the mattress onto the bed frame with Raff on top. It felt like the greatest victory. Wow. Even though we had such a rocky start the night before, surprisingly Raff quickly settled into this new arrangement with all the support. It made things much easier for wound care, bedding changes, and just general comfort. We had no idea that she would not leave that bed again.

The hardest part of the decision to go with hospice was that the treatments came to an end. Our focus changed to comfort versus cure. During these first days under hospice care, we knew that her calcium levels were rising. I ran the scenario in my head. Eventually her neurological symptoms would begin to show up, as they had the past three times we took laps around that torturous track. She would have to endure the car, the hospital, the treatment, and then the car ride back.

In the days after her fall, Raff asked when her next infusion would be and I froze. There was no next infusion because treatment stops when hospice starts. We had discussed that with the hospice intake nurse. Did Raff not remember? Why was she asking? The tumors were growing and we were losing the battle. The treatment we had chosen could not outpace the rapid growth of these vicious tumors. I had been crystal clear in our earlier hospice conversation that I was NOT giving up on her. In no way was I throwing in the towel. I would fight for her forever if that was what our cards were. But in these moments her neurological deficit began to reveal itself, and this realization tore my heart out. I relive this conversation and to be honest, it still haunts me.

Next she asked when she was going to get out of bed, she couldn't be stuck in this bed. But her body was so weak, she had just fallen. She couldn't get out of bed for a while. After seeing so many injuries in my days in the fitness business, I knew that the full effects of her fall were days away. To watch her process that reality was terrible. Crumbled my spirit. To watch the love of my life process that she was really coming to the end was torturous to all that was love inside of me.

She was asleep almost all of the time. These days, she was very tired, for years the tumors had literally consumed her, her body, and all her energy. Her calcium was rising, so the windows of real coherent interaction were closing. I don't know what I expected when I was losing her, but I didn't expect that we would not be able to communicate in our last days together. She just kind of faded away slowly. I had all of these ideas, I wanted to write to the girls with her, I wanted to record videos with her for the girls to watch on their coming birthdays, I wanted to talk with her about all the things, and time just expired. THIS is a f*cking MONSTER to deal with. I can still feel my heart quivering as I write. It was nearly unbearable. I was watching everything I had fought to build all these years just fade away.

At a certain point she was really almost totally unresponsive. There was a deep panic that happened inside me when I saw her go into that moment and saw her struggle. Because of our choice, Do Not Resuscitate (DNR), I would just be there as she crossed over. We agreed there would be no attempt beyond pain meds to medically help her out of the final scenario. This was so hard and so counterintuitive. Our whole lives, when someone got hurt or struggled, we helped them, or got them help. It was basically ingrained in us. And now, I had to turn that off, for the one person I chose to give everything to. The one love of my life. Do I just have to watch this go down? The answer to this unanswerable question was yes, a quivering yes. I just had to watch as it all went down.

I don't remember how many days it was after she became unresponsive until she passed, but it was at least a handful. During these final weeks the family was around constantly, and we all talked with her, held her hand, did absolutely anything we could think of to show her love.

I asked that people send messages to her, printed the messages on colored paper, and taped them on the walls all around the room so she could see them. I wanted to make sure she knew that she was loved. I wasn't sure she could understand what we were saying to her or even how her mind was working, but I knew all of the colors would make her feel some joy. I couldn't fathom her laying there feeling all alone through these days. Writing this, I had to stop multiple times just to type these words. My heart still breaks open thinking about all of it.

| 48 |

Beauty in the Heartbreak

There were moments that were so poignant. As when I watched the girls come in to see Raff to tell her they loved her, that she was a great mother, and how much they cared for her. Ace who at one time couldn't even look at Raff would go in all the time and talk with her. And Rue, who by her nature was a bit more avoidant, was also in there all the time telling her how much she loved her. They would give her kisses. It was in those moments, the blade drew across my heart in a way it never had. My heart bled for my girls, that they were losing their mother. Children should never lose their mothers. But I will tell you, as terrible as all this is, we made the best choice. We weathered the storm together. And I believe our girls are fortified in who they are, and are better off for it. It wasn't and still isn't easy, but I am proud of the path we chose.

It was Tuesday night, before bed, that I thought it was over. I wheeled the hospital bed next to mine, so I could sleep right next to her, hear her breathing, and check that she was okay throughout the night. I must have been awake 42 times. There was no response from her, she was just breathing, labored breathing. We sat with her the entire day on Wednesday. We all thought that would be the last day, too. We took turns talking with her, saying our last words to her, over and over again, not knowing which breath was going to be the last. But her breathing continued through that whole day. That night, I again rolled her bed up to mine to be with her and check in on her; and each time I checked, she was only breathing, labored as it had been for two days, but she made it through that night also.

On Thursday morning at 6 o'clock, I thought this would have to be the end. I was so sure that I kept looking at my watch to see the time. Her labored breathing sometimes became erratic and she would almost miss a breath or two; then there were some shallow breaths, then a big breath, then silence. I would panic, then I would hear her inhale. It was agonizing. I found myself thanking God for her breaths, thanking Him for one more. This all sounded so crazy, because I thought of all the breaths we had together and I don't remember thanking him for any of those, and yet here I was repeating, thank you, over and over.

I love the connection between our breaths and God. Yahweh, the Hebrew word for God. Yahweh, literally means "I AM" and is spoken as we breathe. Take away the vowels and it is YHWH. YH is the inhale, the WH is the exhale. When you are born into this world your first breath is a prayer to God, a recognition that you were made in His image. When you cross over, your last breath is also a prayer to God.

So, as she breathed those last breaths, I thought of us praying; and thought what a beautiful design we are part of. During this last day, she extended her body, and it looked like she was silently roaring. She stretched her body that had been motionless for days, and it appeared she was letting out the most powerful silent roar. She did this five or six times. I didn't know what to think of it at the time, but I believe she was exhibiting her power and her spirit in these last moments. When she gave birth to our first daughter Rue, the roar that came from the pit of her soul was this majestic primal victorious celebration of all that was life. I believe that also happened on that last Thursday. We sat there all day and thought she was done at least 50 times. My heart was exhausted, my body was exhausted, it just swirled with torrents of emotion. We had a house full of people, we were just all crushed, and she was still with us.

That afternoon I decided to pull the girls aside into their room and have the talk I never thought I would have with them. I brought them in, sat down on the bed, and the floodgates opened. My eyes burst with tears. Choking on my words, I said, "Girls, I think we are going to lose Mama soon. She is going to go be with Jesus. If there is anything you would like to say to her, this would be your time. She won't respond, but she can hear you, and she still loves you. No matter what she looks like, she is still your Mama, the same one you remember and love so much." What happened next, I still cannot hardly believe. I extended my arms to them and said, "I'm so sorry my girls." With tear-filled faces they said, "Papa, it's not your fault, you did everything you could." The blessing that these words carried. It's not possible to describe the magnitude of that moment. Then Ace said, "God came to me in a dream. He showed me a cemetery, and told me Mama was going to pass away." She already knew. They hugged me, and I hugged them, and they went in to talk with Mama. I just sat there speechless. Their resilience, and their support of me as their father. They held me together as life pulled me apart.

The sun was low on the horizon and we were still at Raff's bedside stepping out for a quick bite to eat one by one. I had the hardest time eating or doing anything that day, as I felt the time was close. I wanted so desperately to be there when she crossed. It was a blood-curdling scream from the other room that pierced the silence. It was one of the kids. I tapped Raff's sister on the leg as I could tell it was her daughter and she ran out to see what happened, and a few seconds later, I ran out to check. Come to find out our oldest had playfully tossed her cousin at the giant bean bag, but her cousin missed the target, ricocheted off a smaller stuffed animal, and her butt hit the floor. I went out to console Rue who was having a complete breakdown. She had a complete inconsolable breakdown, screamed at the top of her lungs, screamed obscenities into a pillow, complete rage, just totally lost it. She has the biggest heart and hated that her cousin got hurt. And, in the midst of it all she was losing her Mama, a struggle no nine year old should endure. The living room was FULL of tension and emotion and screaming. I was trying my best to keep it together for Raff who was 20 feet away from this fiasco and struggling in the most epic way. I felt so torn because my daughter needed me like no other, and I wanted to be with Raff. The contrast between the energy in one room to the other felt like ice to flames. Everyone had panic in their eyes, everyone was just barely clinging to reality, fever pitch doesn't even come close to describing this moment.

Then it happened. Raff's mom ran out of our room.

"NOW," she said loudly, almost shouting above the chaos.

I put Rue down, and ran to Raff's bedside.

She was gone.

I missed it.

I wasn't there when she crossed

I was so crushed.

The panic was inconceivable. I felt so lost, and just shattered. I stood there just broken into a million pieces. I felt guilt for not being there, I felt gutted at our loss, I felt despair at the concept of life without her. I felt completely numb. There was no question that her spirit had crossed. There was no animation in her body. There was a cold flatness to her body. She was not there. As much as I wanted to hear her breathe just one more time, as much as I wanted to feel her squeeze my hand, she was gone.

I kissed her on her forehead and said my final goodbye. I called the girls into their room again. They knew, and I was devastated as I said, "Mama went to be with Jesus. You are welcome to go see her if you want, but that is your choice." They both went in and we each placed a peony on her body with some other Christmas ornaments the girls made for her. Peonies were Raff's favorite flower, and a bouquet of them sat right next to her for her last days with us. Watching them give a Christmas ornament to their deceased mother was horrid, but was so adorned in beauty.

After the girls said their final words and kissed her we all just kind of tried to just exist for a moment. The ZAP of energy I felt in those few moments was so strange, and I hope that I never feel it again. The silence was deafening, I felt my heartbeat in my neck; it was as if I was overheating and shivering all meshed into one confusing moment.

Her mother described what happened, and then I realized the beauty in all the heartbreak. As we consoled the kids in the other room, her mom had asked Raff what she needed. I had already told Raff that it was ok to go. She didn't need to hang on any longer, we would be okay. Those were the hardest words to tell the love of your life, but I did. In her final moments, I believe she was protecting us, just as she had always done. She didn't want us to be there with her when she passed. She needed space to let go. She loved us too much to let go with us by her side. Her whole life, she always took care of those around here, it was simply how she was wired. All throughout our marriage she gave everything she had to our beautiful daughters and to me. And, in the middle of the storm after that blood-curdling scream she wanted me to be with the girls protecting and comforting them. That's exactly where she would have been if the roles were switched. There was a weird comfort in that realization. I truly believe God gave her just the right amount of breaths to hang on until then. She took her first breath with her mother, and she took her last breath with her mother. To Raff motherhood was her highest honor and privilege, and I have no doubt that is why it all happened in this way.

| 49 |

Disorienting Reality

I never considered what the day after would be like. The day after she passed. The day behind invisible walls of fear. Maybe it had crossed my mind but I really had never let myself go down that path because I chose to hold onto hope, even in the moments after her spirit left her. Perhaps I was naive, but I wasn't going to let myself accept it, until it was final. There was no script, there was no prep, there was only presence the day after, when the raw reality set in; the reality that I didn't choose this, that I didn't want to do this life alone, I didn't want to be a single parent, I didn't want to lose the love of my life. The list goes on and on.

"I want Mama." It's now the dreaded three-word phrase that starts an avalanche of emotion. Tears become sobbing. Then again, "I want Mama." It took only one to say it and both girls teared up. We all did. We all crumbled into a pile of inconsolable grief. And, we were always on that precipice. Any struggle, disagreement, disappointment, frustration, fatigue, even a memory could elicit the three-word phrase. At times I held my breath and prayed that no one said it, knowing what would come, a deep well of grief. And, coming back up out of that pit was hard.

The next days and weeks were a numb, disoriented blur. To have your person gone after spending every day with them for more than 12 years was earth shattering. Friends and family were around and we had holiday plans which kept us occupied. But, it was still incredibly hard, as everyone who came into town anticipated spending time with Raff, and now that was just not in the script. The heartbreak was palatable. The grief sat on the couch with all of us, constantly present. We all had our broken moments with surges of tears, and it was a comfort to all be together, but also a sharp dagger to talk about how Raff would have loved this.

A last minute trip out of town was not in the plan, but it was a welcome distraction from the scalding reality that loomed ahead. So, I pulled together a trip to see my family in Kansas. That time back home gave us support from both family and some select friends who at least allowed us to share the grief. Sharing and crying with each other made those moments survivable. I think I was desperate. I had become completely numb, and wanted to keep myself from checking out completely. I knew holding it all in wasn't the way to go. Thoughts of establishing new holiday traditions for our family was on one hand really terrifying but also an opportunity to plant our flag, claim space in this world for a new chapter, a real coming of age moment. Maybe? With little kids, this small window of time became all too apparent. We had been all over the place for years and years, and in a holding pattern of panic the past five years. Our attempts at tradition had just not taken root. And, now we were without the heart of our family who we looked to for direction. We had no traditions. It felt like we had nothing, except heartbreak.

Most of those days at my parents' house passed in a blur but there was a moment that stopped me in my tracks. You may remember that

Disorienting Reality

many weeks earlier our youngest had told me that God came to her in a dream and He told her Mama was going to pass away. I was so struck by that. Then there was something else. I'm not sure what it revealed, maybe some kind of deep spiritual connection, a clairvoyance maybe? I came across a piece of artwork, made with markers on canvas, an angel beneath bright colorful splashes. Ace created it sometime in 2024 before we left Kansas City in August. My mom discovered it when she was packing the kids' rooms, and she tucked it away as she did so many of the grandkids' masterpieces. However, she knew this artwork was different, deeply meaningful. What struck me most about it was what Ace wrote on the back.

2024 By Ace
Welcome to heaven

Ace KNEW! Immediately my thoughts went back to Ace's dream where God told her Mama was going to pass away. My mind swirled. When did she have that dream? We worried so much about the kids and how to talk to them about what was happening and the possibility of the end. But I think they knew so much more than we thought. They were so plugged in to what was actually happening, far beyond our understanding.

Thank You, Cancer

Looking back to our 10th anniversary in October, I considered that a huge accomplishment; I was so proud of us that we stuck it out as marriage is definitely not for the faint of heart. It was a daily effort, heck it was a moment to moment effort. I was absolutely crushed by how it turned out, where our lives were at that milestone. We were getting absolutely annihilated by cancer. It consumed every waking moment we had. It demanded all of our attention at all hours. So many days riddled with panic and exhaustion, literally years of sleepless nights, wound care and struggle, we were just cooked. We had been in triage mode for longer than I can remember.

I was standing in the living room of our new home, the one that we worked so hard for. We had nothing in the house yet. Just empty space awaiting us. Raff slowly inched out of our bedroom. She had a fluffy green blanket wrapped around her. Despite being so thin and bent over from all the pain and exhaustion, she told me that she loved the house, that it was a great way to celebrate our 10th anniversary, and that it would be a great house to heal in.

When she said those words, a waterfall of emotion erupted from my heart and cascaded down to my toes. I felt like I spilled out all over the room. I had tried so hard, I had hoped and prayed, and we had gone against all odds to land this place. Everything in me was heartbroken for our lives, but she found joy in that moment and that memory makes the waterfall continue.

Upon reflection, I could also see a deeper meaning in her words. She had said this would be a good place to heal. Obviously, I attributed that to her, to her healing from all those torturous years. I'll never know for sure, but perhaps she also thought about the girls and me as well, about her family healing. Throughout our life together her focus was always on our healing. She constantly was on me about this and that, trying to optimize my health. In light of that, perhaps her words that night went beyond the bounds of what I saw at that moment. This home would be a great place for the girls and me to heal also. In that house she did heal. She was relieved of the suffering. Her cancer came to an end. She is not in pain any more. And now it would be our turn to heal. To walk this path in a different way, but with healing as the focus. I believe her statement was a reflection of our love for one another and our love for our family. What a gift her words were.

In January 2025 we returned to the emptiness of our home in Texas, and reality began to set in. The quiet moments were the worst. The moments where we had the urge to go talk to her. The moments when we woke up, and when we went to bed, that was when the war began. Navigating that in my heart was one thing, but the girls had their own experiences, and holding space for them as well took everything I had most days. The slippery slope to a dark downward spiral happened at least once per day, many days more. It showed up when everyone was tired, it showed up when someone was hungry, it showed up in disagreements and inconveniences, it just came and grabbed us by our throats and throttled us. For example, the girls would get into an argument over typical sister stuff, I would step in and do the parent thing, and try to help them find a solution to whatever was happening. They can't seem to reach a resolution and the disagreement moves to tantrum level. Then I get upset because they won't cooperate or even attempt to find a solution. Then, the downward spiral starts. "I want Mama, I miss Mama, I want to hug Mama." There was no solution to that, and by then, everyone was so over it, the issue that was paramount had been completely forgotten. Yet I found myself still upset, and had to somehow build an emotional bridge to comfort them. I cannot put into words how challenging it was for us, and it seems that it has happened 1000 times; it should be getting easier, yet it is still such a mountain.

The emptiness in the house was overwhelming. Raff was at home when she passed, so in nearly every space there are memories of her. I consider it a gift from God that we all still very much want to live here. No one feels weird about it, we all genuinely like this home. I can envision tons of scenarios where that wouldn't be the case. Yet, the emptiness was hard to manage. To help fill the void with joyful memories, I created photo collages for a Mama wall. In the previous photo, Raff is wrapped in a fluffy green blanket in front of a big wall. That big wall became our Mama wall. It displays more than 600 photos with MAMA in 12" letters mounted above. It is the centerpiece in our house, and I find myself sitting right there every day. It fills that empty space with memories, laughs, and our love. I'm thankful for that.

School also helped to fill the emptiness when we returned home. The girls had never attended a full-time school, a five-days-a-week school, because we chose the homeschool co-op route. I was mortified as I anticipated this transition. Before they started school in January, I let the teachers and the school counselor know. But even at that, when I took them to school those first few days I literally couldn't even speak without breaking down in tears. Thankfully they took to school like fish to water. The school counselor even started a grief support group for the girls with a couple other students who had lost their mother. The school turned out to be a tremendous gift and such a welcome path for them. They loved it. Between the school and their church home, the girls feel safe, have friends, and we are rebuilding our lives from the wreckage.

| 50 |

Love Transcends Death

This may be obvious, but I really struggled with the fact that Raff was just simply not present. I didn't feel her energy, and this was slowly, silently gutting me in the weeks and months after her passing. She was my best friend. I loved so much to say, "Hey, Babe." I just adored talking with her, laughing at jokes with her, and making romantic passes at her. And, I couldn't do that anymore. It was like the well-worn path of engaging with her was now grown over and disappeared. That loss was ruining me moment by moment. I wasn't really vocal about it, I was just trying to survive.

I got a message one day from the gal who donated the stay at her river house. Renee, who had six kids and had also lost her spouse to cancer. We had stayed in touch a bit but only from a distance during Raff's last weeks and months. There was always something I didn't really want to put out into the universe. When someone reached out to me who had lost a spouse, something inside me kept a distance from that relationship. I think because I didn't want to admit to myself that it could be me who lost my spouse. I wasn't rude or anything, I just didn't really make much of an effort to interact with that person. I guess I was so afraid of breaking Raff's spirit and wanted her to know without question that we all stood behind her and with her for her healing. I did not want to give any sign that I thought it was over. I just couldn't bear the thought of failing her.

> But here I was, in the depths of grief, lost, struggling, barely *lifeing*, and she messaged, "Can I send you a Book?" She said it wasn't some basic grief book. I was intrigued because she had literally been in my shoes since losing her husband two years ago. So sure, I would take a look at it. A few days later the book *Signs* came in the mail. *Signs* is all about communicating with those who have crossed over. The woman who wrote it, Laura Lynne Jackson, is a psychic which threw up a red flag for me. My only filter, our only filter, in this journey had been Jesus. Our trust was in Him, and if it didn't jive with Him, I was out. But, in the book she addresses that exact issue. She matter-of-factly explained her skill set just like anybody else's skill set, and that it could be used for God or against Him. The author described your person who crossed as a member of your very own Team of Light. She said your person joins angels and archangels who are there to help you throughout your life, and God reigns above all of these angelic beings. In light of this explanation, I was a bit more open to what I was reading.

As I got further into the book, I found that the stories were comforting me in a way I never imagined. There were very few people who I knew that had an experience similar to mine, so this book broadened my lens to include others who were in my same space. Further on, the book covered communication with your person, and your Team of Light. Because your person and this team don't occupy the same physical space, her contention was that we need to become aware of their communications because they were sending signs all the time. The key was to be open to them, because those signs can happen outside of our five senses or they come across on a different frequency. Her suggestion was to simply ask your person to clearly communicate

Love Transcends Death

with you, which I immediately did. I laid down on my bed, closed my eyes, and asked Raff to let me know she was here. The next step was to establish how you would know it was your person and not just some random coincidence. I thought about this a bit, and Raff's favorite animal was an elephant, so I figured if she wanted to get me a message, maybe I would see an elephant somehow. Maybe it would be a sticker, or on social media, or a TV show, or a billboard, or maybe an elephant would walk by; but somehow her communication would be apparent and beyond coincidence because of the elephant, just like the picture on the back cover of this book. I also thought maybe she would use a smiley face, because she so loved sewing smiles on jackets and pants and shirts. This all sounded so crazy and far-fetched. That was about all the thought I gave it before I was drawn away to make dinner or attend to something else domestic like that.

In spite of how crazy and far-fetched the ideas in *Signs* seemed, within two hours or so I received a message from Dr. Jess, Raff's chiropractor, cancer survivor, and literally Raff's soul sister. I told Dr. Jess weeks before that when I speak with her, I literally feel like Raff is there with us. Something just connects. There is an undeniable energy. The message she sent included a video clip of singer Brandon Lake, a Christian artist, whose music I love. The song is *Don't You Give Up On Me*.

Don't lose your hope
Don't lose your faith
That's where your fight is

I got more dreams
I got more plans
I got more blessings

Open your heart
Open your hands
Open your eyelids

I've got more dreams
I've got more plans
I've got more blessings

These words literally spoke to the deepest concerns and fears that I had at the moment. I hadn't shared these fears with anyone. I had definitely not shared them with Dr. Jess. The only person who may have known these things would have been Raff, and I don't recall if I had shared them with her.

When I heard those words, I thought they were literally written for me. I couldn't believe this message. I was mortified at what life even meant now or what life had in store after such a great loss. I didn't want to do life, not that I was going to end mine or anything like that, I just had no gusto, I had no desire for wanting to see tomorrow. The only thing keeping me going was the responsibility of my girls. I literally had to drag myself through the days.

Then, there was more. Dr. Jess typed out lines of text that would have only come from Raff. The words she said pointed directly at my pain. She said them as Raff would have delivered them, and there was no way Jess would have known to say these things. My jaw hit the floor again. "Don't you think for a second that she wants you living life at half speed. FULL SEND. It's who she fell in love with and who she still loves. BIG Energy, Big Dreams. Her Investment into your life cannot be wasted. Do something with your sadness. SHE IS WITH YOU. You can't see her but she is there."

These words couldn't have come at a better moment. And, Dr. Jess was the perfect person to deliver. Was it because of our shared love for Raff? I don't know. When I thanked her for the messages I asked why she had sent them. She said that she knew that she should. I couldn't believe it. It was within hours of me asking for clear communication from Raff. Is that what was happening or was this another answered prayer? Here We Are. That night I went to bed laughing and reeling over the happenings. It was clear to me that God used Dr. Jess to send messages I so desperately needed.

A side note regarding the song lyrics: As this book was being edited, I became aware of the possibility of copyright violations for including song lyrics. I immediately went to social media and reached out to the songwriters to get their permission to print the lyrics. I know it sounds crazy, and I kid you not, but within 40 minutes I received a message back from one of them who said, "It's truly why we do it. We're honored that you would include the song in your book." Thank you Brandon Lake, Michael Fatkin, and Benjamin William Hastings for your talents and for allowing me to keep your fine words in this book. Another moment in our story where God made light work of what could have been an insurmountable hurdle.

The next morning I woke up to a message on Instagram from another friend of Raff's. She proceeded to tell me that she was not sure if it was too soon, but she wanted to introduce me to someone. She sent the profile of a guy who lost his wife to cancer in 2020. He has three children, wrote a book after his wife passed, and started his own publishing company. Now, I appreciated the introduction, but what made it unbelievably remarkable was that she didn't know that I had always wanted to write a book, nor did she know that Raff and I talked about writing one together. She didn't know that I began writing *Thank you, Cancer* three days before she messaged me. She also had no idea that the week before I had called a friend who had published a book asking a bunch of publishing questions. Nor did she know that writing a book is the ONLY thing I am sure I should do with my life right now. I thanked her for the wildly, well-timed introduction to that publisher, who ultimately became my publisher. I think I laughed and cried all at the same time.

After all that, she then told me a detail she had forgotten. Back in 2020, when she learned that her friend, the publisher's wife, had passed, she was with Raff at the elephant exhibit at the zoo. My mind exploded. An elephant. I had decided 15 hours earlier that an elephant would be an undeniable link to communication from Raff. I didn't tell anyone

> about it. Raff's friend could not have known about the connection to the elephant. This moment, this path was set into motion in 2020, five years earlier, at the elephant exhibit when Raff's friend got the news of a friend's passing. It was nearly impossible to deny the whole experience was woven by the hand of God. I still can feel the moment all this happened. The love that pulses through my body even after she is gone, continues to light a path for me these days. A love of this magnitude can only come from God. It transcends death. An undying love.

I just sat there and cried. It was overwhelming. Those messages were just what I needed. I felt her presence all around me. You may think it is all too wild to be true, and maybe it is too wild for you, but, it wasn't too wild for me. Everything changed on that day. I opened my heart, opened my hands, opened my eyelids to a grander experience, and everything expanded. Ever since this day, I have felt more like myself, I have felt a renewal of spirit, I have felt motivated to re-engage with life. It didn't fix everything, but it did change everything.

There are a few things I want to address about these experiences. The first being the undeniable evidence of God leading us forward in this whole story. He continually lights our path forward, and I believe He met me in my grief and delivered the comfort I so desperately needed. Rumi, the 13th century Persian poet said it well, "The wound is the place where the light enters you." I attribute all of these messages to God's grace that covered me at this time. He saw me and used specific people to deliver messages to me. These experiences are mine and are highly subjective. I believe our perspective informs our perception. I continually lean into God for his provision, and that's what I would pass along to you. I tell you these stories as messages of hope. God is not limited by our formula or our understanding, and He knows no bounds. He will meet you where you are. If you are engaged with God, the communication and comfort you receive will look different than mine; it will be more true to your relationship with your loved one. My offering is that you stay hopeful, and you keep that hope before God.

At this time, I also cannot deny the immense vulnerability in my heart, and the tendency to grasp at anything that seems to offer peace. We can't ignore the opportunity to be led astray. A wounded heart is a tremendous opportunity for the darkness. Guard your heart. Keep your eyes set on Jesus.

Signs was a very aptly named signpost that brought me communication and comfort in the right moment through God's Grace. Each of the participants in these messages had a clear connection to Him. Despite my initial skepticism, I came to see His hand in all of this as time went on. Once again, these are my experiences. An elegant tapestry woven by the Creator Himself.

> "For my thoughts are not your thoughts, neither are your ways my ways," declares the LORD.
> "As the heavens are higher than the earth, so are my ways higher than your ways and my thoughts than your thoughts." Isaiah 55:8-9

Through Scripture, we see Him speak through a donkey, bring dead bones to life, collapse the walls of Jericho with the army's band, stop the sun so the Israelites could win a battle, speak through various means, and more importantly, bring our Savior through a virgin's birth, a Savior who also does remarkably supernatural works, dies, is buried, rises from the dead, and ascends to Heaven and is still alive.

We all go through this life and our experiences occur within our own little boxes. Whether you realize it or not, your experiences do too. Your box looks different from mine, because we are all unique, but our little boxes or worlds sit next to and around everyone else's little worlds. Unfortunately, the more we become connected to such things as social media, phones, technology, etc, the more disconnected and detached our boxes render our lives. But, what I hadn't really considered is forced expansion. By this I mean that life will present you with scenarios that leave you only two choices, stay in the box you're in or expand out of your box and into a whole new space, I'll call the new space a map. Outside of all of our little boxes is a map that contains more, more of everything. An expanded version of our experience.

Furthermore, I think that the bounds of the map are not the end either. There is a territory that contains all the maps. I believe when these expansive events happen, you begin to see that our understanding of our experiences doesn't hold a candle to the grand design of our God who stitched all of this together. And this experience is not the only one. The bounds that sprawl off into the everythingness of creation, house all the territories, and for this, we'll have to talk to our Creator.

It was in the grief of losing Raff that I came upon information that opened my eyes. I could never have imagined the day after she passed, yet here I am. And very true to her expression and her path, Here We Are, a business name we never really built out while she was here, but it still holds true and I will carry it as a torch to honor our union. In this torturous time, my eyes were opened to more. The little box I was living in was blown wide open.

I was writing this book on a dreary cold morning, writing about her very last breath and that tear-filled moment, then the sun blasted through the thick cloud cover and bathed me in the warmest sunshine. It was exactly synced up as I typed the words. Some may call this coincidence. Maybe those people don't know that Raff worshiped the sunshine. She would stop mid-sentence and turn her head to the sun and close her eyes, and just sit there for long periods of time. We chuckled at her in Arizona thinking that she just wanted to be a lizard on a rock. Maybe they don't know that this burst of sunshine came when the sun had been hidden behind the clouds for days. Maybe those people have not experienced a once-in-a-lifetime love that turned into a loss, that transcended this physical space. Maybe those people are still frittering time away within the walls of the little box they are not even aware of. Maybe they have not openly sat with pain and yearned for connection across a bridge that they could not see. Maybe they don't know that I am sitting at home on a couch in front of the Mama wall with collages of more than 600 pictures of our lives with Raff. I'll consider that sun-drenched moment as a sign from Raff. That she was holding me. She was right here, and she was letting me know. The girls and I will continue to stand in the morning sunshine and say hi to Mama.

Love Transcends Death

A few days later, I was talking with my mother-in-law, laughing about how hard-headed Raff was, how she would just not budge for anyone unless she understood and agreed. I had to laugh because at the top of a tree, 50 feet above the ground, a candy apple red cardinal was literally laughing. It's call sounded just like a deep guttural laugh, just like the moment I fell in love with Raff. The bird was so loud, my mother-in-law laughed. It would not let up, for at least two to three minutes this cardinal was going to town. At that moment, I knew she was telling us that she was there.

I get so many messages. Just yesterday I got a message from a family friend that became very close to us in Raff's last season and was just an angel walking with our family. She sent me a video from a singer named Danny, who sang a song he wrote when he lost his wife, *Letting Your Heart Beat Again*. I took that as no coincidence either. In fact, she said that she felt compelled to send it to me after viewing one of my posts about Raff on social media. I cried as I listened to the song, as I do many that remind me of Raff. But this one came as a timely message, that really seemed like something Raff would have said. Another friend messaged me in the weeks following Raff's passing, when I was very distraught and rattled about the whole experience. This friend sent me a music video after she saw one of my Instagram posts. In my post Raff and I were dancing and celebrating in a pasture following some great news about her condition. In the message my friend sent there was an album cover, a photograph of the artist in an identical pasture scene. The title song on the album is *She's Alright*.

Love that turns to loss, can turn back to love. A mighty love like Raff and I had resulted in a mighty loss. There are just times we will find ourselves in loss. It's unavoidable, part of the human condition. The magnitude of the loss is a function of your tolerance. So to compare loss from one to the other is a fool's errand. In this light, those of us who have experienced loss have a connection, and that's what matters. Our loss mirrors our love. It's there because you were blessed with the love you know so well. I stumbled upon a quote that really changed my experience.

Thank You, Cancer

Grief is all of the unspent love you carry for the one you lost - Andrew Garfield

The weight of everything I felt was because her passing was like a cork stuck in the faucet of love that I had turned on full blast. I felt the build up. There was nowhere to release all that love now that she was gone. I was confused, I felt heavy, I was angry, I was many other things. When I realized that this heavy feeling was a resource to spend, everything changed. For me, writing was always a haven, I was able to process so much by putting words to a page. It helped release the pressure. It also allowed me to express my love for Raff. I post videos and reminisce with all of you about all the love we shared. I watch her laugh and I just melt. I am writing this book which fulfills a dream we both had, and that shares the legacy of our love. I am able to remove the cork and let that love flow. It's not like it was, but it's the same love. It has a familiar feeling to it. I feel like a different human when I write. The messages I receive from all of you bring her back for a moment.

You may not be a writer, maybe you like the driving range, maybe puzzles, maybe sewing. It doesn't really matter. Those things that connected you with your person are ways to share the love you still have, not that you had, but you have. Because love is bigger than the here and now. Our bodies fail. Love comes from our immortal God, and friends we may never know its expanse. But I will tell you this, going through this experience has given me proof that there is more. And if you lean in, it will lead you forward.

| 51 |

I Wasn't Afraid to Die Anymore

I used to think of death as the end. It's all done. Game over. And then I went through this. These moments have been so connected with her. I heard it described in such an eloquent way. Someone held up a piece of paper to hide what was on the other side. The paper represented death. There's no question that there are things on the other side of this paper that cannot be seen. And to those that have not experienced death from a close perspective, it may seem an impassable obstacle. But my experience has taught me this piece of paper is actually just a doorway. And there is more.

What if we weren't so shaken by death? What if we weren't afraid? Now, I can't say I arrived at this all by myself. When cancer struck the first time, Raff and I found ourselves DEEP in conversations we never dreamed we'd have, well at least at that early juncture in our lives together. During this journey Raff made multiple laps around the coming- to-terms-with-your-mortality track. I am in awe of the travels she made internally during these years. On the other hand I was there by her side, and, in comparison, made just small steps in that direction. But that was always an open conversation in our house. Over the years our inability to deal with surface relationships became very apparent due to the depth of common talks like this.

It was a pretty normal day for us in Scottsdale during Raff's months of treatment there. The girls and I were driving down Scottsdale Road after we just left our favorite coffee shop in the Scottsdale Quarter. We were headed down to a park for a bit while Raff was in treatment for the day. My head was nowhere in particular, it was just another day of the week inside this odd existence we were in. Then a thought hit me, *I wasn't afraid to die any more*. I don't know why it came up, but it was like a billboard in my mind. It was like God placed it there. I didn't try to arrive there. I just found myself there. I didn't have fear around it any more, and what an unexpected liberating gift it was.

Now, I don't want to leave this life anytime soon. I want to do more things in my life. I want to walk my girls down the aisle if they choose to get married. I used to want to grow old with Raff. There was so much more I looked forward to. And possibly the most important part of all this was that I was exactly where I wanted to be. I could not imagine a place on earth where my time was more valuable. Maybe my greatest contribution existed in those moments. I knew in the pit of my soul, that I was moving IN PURPOSE, and this was a tremendous sigh of relief. It didn't make it easy, but it refortified my foundation. I knew I was with my person, Raff and I were just magic, that relationship brought a harmony to my life that I never could have imagined. Wherever this path led, I knew this was the one I was supposed to be on. If it all ended, I was ok with that.

When the path made the turn I didn't choose, when Raff crossed, in the disorienting tailspin that was the next few months I had a conversation with my girls that still takes my breath away. We were talking about Mama, as we do every day. Some days it's laughs, most days it's tears. But on this day, while we were driving, Ace said, "Papa, I'm not afraid of dying."

"Oh yeah?" I asked.

"Yeah, I will get to see Mama."

I choked up and said, "Yes, you will."

Rue chimed in, "I'm not afraid either. I just don't want the pain."

"Fair point, me either love."

These two girls have gone through unimaginable loss before they saw their 10th birthdays. They have comforted me many times. As an example, when they are breaking down, if they see me cry they immediately stop their own unraveling and come to hug me. They talked to Raff when she was non-responsive and told her how much they loved her. The gravity of these conversations and the courage in their hearts to do that was awe inspiring. And here they are explaining to me how they don't fear death. The resilience and the emotional latitude of these girls is breathtaking. They are their mother's daughters, they carry her wild spirit within them.

Could you imagine if we, I'm talking about you and me, the adults here, grew up with that type of mindset. In a world shackled with fear, could you imagine what would be possible with that perspective? A Bonus Mindset, as if today is a Bonus. We get another day to keep on the path we were made for. Operating IN PURPOSE. We can do more with our lives. We can write another page of our tremendous stories. We have been given this gift.

We have had family in town for various reasons since Raff passed, and it has an air of heartbreak to it. I have to tell you about a moment that happened in preparation for Rue's 10th birthday. This is a year of firsts, first time doing celebrations without Mama. It's a glaring nightmare that won't leave. The domestic tasks are not my favorite to put it lightly, nor do I feel prepared to host events. That was more of Raff's forte. I was making the bed upstairs for her step-mom to come and stay and as I draped the final sheet across the bed, I heard Raff say "Thanks, Babe." I didn't hear it audibly, but I heard it. I can't explain it with any more clarity, but since she passed, my attunement to her messages has heightened. And, again, that is what changed everything for me. I just laughed and carried on with my day. Another pristine example of love transcending death. Another gift from God.

If there is one take away for you from all of this, I would urge you to lean into your relationship with God. Talk to him like a friend. He's there, I have never been more sure of this in my life. I have been a part of the church in some respect my whole life, but this time has brought me so close to Him, in a way I have never experienced. We, silly humans, believe we have control. There is so much more to this life.

"Are not five sparrows sold for two pennies? Yet not one of them is forgotten by God. Indeed, the very hairs of your head are all numbered. Don't be afraid; you are worth more than many sparrows." Luke 12:6-7

If we reframe death, why not talk about it like the doorway that it is. When your love continues past the day you so fear, it begs the question, what else is there that I do not know? It wouldn't make sense that such a surplus of love just goes to waste, or just evaporates away. Where does this surplus come from? Therein lies the transcendent nature of love. And thus the connection to God. It wasn't until I watched the love of my life disappear from my reality that the majesty of the Resurrection became so clear. To look at your someone who holds the key to your heart laying there after their spirit is gone shatters the fiber of your soul. To think, Jesus lay lifeless for days, crucified at that, and then rose from the grave. In all scenarios He beat death. How can we not live a hallelujah, walking in grace for all the days we are granted?

There were so many times in our journey the next step was unclear. It seemed we were on a stepping stone with the tips of our noses in a dense fog. There was no path in view. It was clear we had to make a move, without seeing or knowing the outcome, and trust God for His provision which continually showed through all of you. A step was required, a step of faith. The answer was not there unless we made the move.

My hope is that you see the undeniable stack of evidence that He showed up for us every single step of the way. I learned the difference between "How can I create a solution?" and "How can I show up fully for His solution?" The difference was in the posture of my heart.

Where do you begin? Do you begin by psyching yourself up in the mirror in the morning? Or, do you begin with Him?

Thank you for reading our story. Thank you for walking this season with us. Raff was very clear that she did not want to be known for cancer, and undeniably she was so much more. She was an expanse of love and joy that I never could have imagined. It's very important to us that this be a story of hope, resilience, and the power of love despite alarming odds.

I've struggled with the conclusion of this book for longer than I care to admit. In talking with some very dear people in my life, I believe I have begun to see some clarity. I was having trouble accepting the fact that our story is over. In my heart and my mind, I just simply don't believe that to be true. The love we shared is still here, I feel it pouring out of me every day. I feel it in my relationships, I feel it from our children, I feel it deep within my being. The love I became so accustomed to in my day to day became a great loss, but in that loss, in that valley, I discovered hope I never knew existed. God met me there. He was holding me in the grief, His love was renewing me in the grief. This love sprouted into a hope that has slowly begun to reveal a path forward. This love I speak about is God's. Our story is a glimpse of the love He has for us, and through His son He opened up our path beyond the feared doorway that is death.

Our cross country journey began back in 2018. That was when we heard the random lady say, "Jesus is with you." We didn't understand then. I get it now.

May this story, our story and experience of heartbreak but also pure JOY, community, love, deep deep healing, parenting through chronic illness, marriage in the face of a heavy diagnosis, freedom in acceptance, the reality of a cancer diagnosis in America—may all these topics and conversations bring light.

- Raffaella Dobles

My final request is that you remember Raff as the marvelous woman she was, not for this struggle or this cancer chapter. Her strength and resilience were breathtaking. She brought an expanse of love, connection, and joy into this world that left an indelible mark on so many. May we always hold on to these loving memories of her in our lives. She brought out the best in those around her. May we honor her memory by showing up as the best that lives within us. May the magnificent ripple she left in this life continue far beyond any imaginable bounds.

With Gratitude

I want to offer a heartfelt thank you to so many people for making this journey possible, for making this story possible. It took legions of amazing humans to bring you the stories emblazoned on these pages. Without all of you, none of this would have come to be.

- To Raff's family - The Masonis, Dobles, Ottavianos, and Roberts, becoming a part of your family and sharing your Raffi has expanded my life in ways I never knew possible. Your generosity, love, and support will always stand as a beacon of your love for Raffi and our family. Raffi wanted so dearly for her family to all be together. During this season, there were no hurdles too great. You all showed up in such an incredible way.

- To my Mom and Dad - I simply don't have the words to express my thanks. To say we felt supported in all of this would fall way short. You made us feel held in all the waves that came our way. This journey, this book would not be what they are without your endless showing up. Thank you and I love you.

- To Brandon and the team at Blue Hat Publishing - Thank you for coming alongside me to bring this book to the world. You all are tremendous.

- To Cory - For your inspiration and leadership in bringing God's voice to this text, I thank you. You're an old friend in a new season of life.

- To our friends - You have become family throughout this journey. At the risk of missing a name, I trust that you know who you are. You have given so generously.

- To everyone who gave in so many ways - through GoFundMe, prayer, meals, help with moving, care for the girls, phone calls, messages, and hugs. By sharing your homes, sharing our story, donating time and talents, and continually sharing memories on social media. I could never thank you in a manner that did justice to our vast appreciation for you. I feel it deep in my heart, it's a surge of warmth. There is and was so much beauty and magic in our story, despite the pain and that struggle, and it can all be attributed to you and your individual contributions.

- Finally, I give thanks to God. This story went way beyond the bounds of our capacity or tolerance. In Him we found strength. In His grace we found a well lit path. In my overwhelming desire to help my wife, I found Him. When there was no hope, no possible solutions, but He spoke through so many of you. He met us in our struggle and so beautifully wove our path together with yours.

You all granted us five years to fight for Raff with everything we had. We could have lost her at the onset in 2020, but because of you all, our girls got to know their mother, our girls got to see just how strong and wonderful their mother was, and I got five more years with the love of my life.

If you found this book impactful, please take a moment and leave a review on Amazon.

This will help it find its way to someone who is searching for light in their darkness.

We had no map when our world fell apart. Raffi found the shift first — quietly, before either of us had words for it, and we forged the path together, one painful step at a time. What emerged was a pattern as old as struggle itself, one that unites every person who has ever had to choose forward in the dark. I want to offer that to you, if you're open to it. This is that pattern, distilled into something you can hold.

Bring Danny to Your Next Event

Danny Lesslie is an author, speaker, and coach.
He and his girls currently reside in Texas.

Requests to speak at
your next company, conference, or church event
should be directed to
www.dannylesslie.co

Follow him at
Instagram - @dannylesslie

www.ingramcontent.com/pod-product-compliance
Lightning Source LLC
Chambersburg PA
CBHW050856160426
43194CB00011B/2179